MORE
CHICAGO HAUNTS
Scenes from Myth and Memory

Ursula Bielski

First Edition

LAKE CLAREMONT PRESS

4650 North Rockwell Street • Chicago, IL 60625
www.lakeclaremont.com

More Chicago Haunts: Scenes from Myth and Memory
by Ursula Bielski

Published October, 2000 by:

4650 N. Rockwell St.
Chicago, IL 60625
773/583-7800; lcp@lakeclaremont.com
www.lakeclaremont.com

Copyright © 2000 by Ursula Bielski

Publisher's Cataloging-in-Publication
(Provided by Quality Books, Inc.)

Bielski, Ursula.
   More Chicago haunts : scenes from myth and memory /
Ursula Bielski. — 1st ed.
   p. cm.
   Includes bibliographic references and index.
   LCCN: 00-107838
   ISBN: 1-893121-04-6

   1. Ghosts—Illinois—Chicago. 2. Haunted house—
Illinois—Chicago. 3. Chicago (Ill.)—History.
4. Chicago (Ill.)—Folklore. I. Title.

B1472.U6B55 2000   133.1'09773'11
                          QBI00-807

**Printed in the United States of America by United Graphics,
an employee-owned company based in Mattoon, Illinois.**

04 03 02   10 9 8 7 6 5 4 3

For AJB—

*who knows that the weirdest
things of all are usually true,
and who keeps looking
for Chicago when the
rest of us despair.*

PUBLISHER'S CREDITS

Cover design by Timothy Kocher. Cover photo of the recovering
of a victim from the *Eastland* disaster, 1915, courtesy of the Chicago
Public Library. Interior design by Sharon Woodhouse. Layout by Ken
Woodhouse and Sharon Woodhouse. Editing by Bruce Clorfene.
Proofreading by Sharon Woodhouse, Karen Formanski, Jason Fargo,
and Ken Woodhouse. Index by Karen Formanski. The text of *More
Chicago Haunts* was set in Times New Roman with heads in
Copperplate Gothic Bold and Viner Hand ITC.

CONTENTS

PREFACE

The book you are about to read is a storybook of sorts.

Unlike the first volume of *Chicago Haunts*, which tripped lightly over the city's history in search of folktales, legends, and even mere rumors of the unknown, the pages ahead are filled with personal experiences of the phantoms in question, often in the observer's own words. Where the witnesses were willing, I've included their true names. Most agreed to full disclosure, though a few opted for anonymity, with little or no harm done to the tales.

Those in search of chapters will find none. These accounts were collected by a listener bombarded with eager storytellers, not by a writer with an outline to flesh out. In presenting them in a random sequence, I hoped to effect in the reader some of the same wonderment—at both their unity and diversity—as I felt when I first heard them, one upon the other, in a rush of words.

Though these stories are, in one way, intended to entertain, the reader would do well to remember that the written testimonies included are not the work of the author, interpreting the experiences of others, but verbatim accounts authored—and signed—by the witnesses themselves.

I think you'll agree that, especially in light of this fact, they are haunting tales indeed.

Acknowledgments

Were it not for the overwhelming response to the first volume of *Chicago Haunts: Ghostlore of the Windy City*, this book would never have been written. The grueling and extensive, complicated, frustrating, and even depressing task of compiling a lifetime's worth of rumors, legends, and experiences of the supernatural—both mine and others'—into a readable volume was one that, in the fall of 1997, I had no intention of ever repeating. With the revision of that first volume in the summer of 1998, after a number of printings, I thought I was done forever with writing in the genre termed by catalogers, publishers, and bookdealers "true regional ghost stories."

Was I wrong.

In the months and years that followed the release of *Chicago Haunts*, I received countless calls, letters, and e-mail posts alerting me to a wide and varied assortment of reported hauntings, visions, poltergeist disturbances, and *psi* occurrences that were going on—some with great frequency and/or reliability—right now, right here, in the city once called "the biggest ghost town in America." In addition, a number of historians both amateur and professional eagerly passed on aging tales from the city's history to add to my own collection of so-called ghostlore.

First and absolutely foremost, I am grateful beyond words to all those who took the time, effort, and energy to track me down and share their stories, whether in person, over the phone, in cards, letters, or on Post-it notes, or in brief or lengthy e-mails to my attention. Nearly half of the accounts included here contain verbatim written testimonies to various phenomena. In this chaotic age, I salute the patience and care of these witnesses who found the time and energy to write down their experiences, and of those who were gracious enough to participate in telephone interviews or to tape record their narratives for me. Though I have credited many of these individuals at the end of their stories that follow, some have remained anonymous or have asked to have their names substituted with imaginary ones in the interest of privacy. As such, I hesitate to overtly thank here these unnamed contributors. Know, however, that your kindliness is often in my thoughts.

Besides those who willingly came forward with their own anecdotes, I am also deeply indebted to those who supplied me with information, leads, encouragement, and other aid as I followed threads provided by others, or who offered tips for possible new tales, including Mike Bratta, Adalbert Bielski, Irene Hughes, Joe Troiani, Nancy Zingrone, Rick Kogan, Michael Fassbender, Mickey Gould, Richard Lindberg, Fr. Julian von Duerbeck, Mike Alft, Barbara Kroner, Wallace Griffith, Dorothy Marcuson, Cardinal Francis George, Dennis William Hauck, Tom Hawes, Jamie Clemons, Frances Kathrein, Bev Ottaviano, Fr. Dennis O'Neill, Jerry Karczewski, Christopher Varney, Tony Romano and the students of Fremd High School, Colin Cordwell, Gregory Singleton, the St. Charles Heritage Center, the Villa Park, Elmhurst, Northfield, and Lombard public libraries, the Music Box Theatre, the Norwood Park Historical Society, the Field Museum, Navy Pier, Cantigny Park, White Cemetery, the Maxwell Street Historic Preservation Coalition, the Divine Word Foundation, the Arlington Heights Historical Association, the Chicago Cubs, Independence Grove Forest Preserve, the Boy Scouts of America, the Billy Goat Tavern, the Bucktown Pub, St. Ignatius College Prep, the Gold Star Bar, the Fireside and its patrons, Camp Fort Dearborn, Rosehill Cemetery, the John Hancock building, the Water Tower Visitors Information Center, the *Chicago Tribune*, Wal-Mart, and, for key information and supporting photographs, the Conrad Sulzer Regional Library, the Chicago Historical Society, and the Chicago Public Library.

I am both encouraged by and encouraging of the ongoing and constant efforts of my fellow regional "ghosthunters," including Richard Crowe, Dale Kaczmarek, Troy Taylor, Dylan Clearfield, Howard Heim, Norman Basile, Bruce Nicholson, and the various regional societies and clubs devoted to investigating spontaneous *psi* phenomena (many of whom have provided their thoughts on purported activity at various sites); and I am daily comforted and cheered by David Cowan, Dolores Bielski, and Adalbert J. Bielski, all of whom were constantly on the lookout for ways to make this book better and my going easier. I am even appreciative of little Eva Cowan, who tried so hard to keep her mom from finishing this project, but who is so darling that one cannot hold it against her.

Without the good folks at Lake Claremont Press, particularly Sharon Woodhouse, I would still be scribbling in notebooks, and everyone would still think I was crazy. For printing my work and at least partially restoring my reputation, I am ever thankful. Along with Sharon, I applaud the gruesome toil of Bruce Clorfene, who spared readers the bulk of my insufferably awful alliterations (there I go again) through his heroic editorial skills; Tim Kocher, whose cover designs just get better and better; Ken Woodhouse, who hand-delivered key documents when my deadline loomed and duties kept me home; and all the hard-working, creative, and enthusiastic others that helped assure a finished product from a mere manuscript.

In addition to those who contributed to both volumes of *Chicago Haunts* either directly or indirectly, I am profoundly grateful to all the librarians, reporters, radio and television people, documentary makers, and others who have seen fit to look to me when they sought an expert on supernatural Chicago. In addition to validating my work enormously, this just keeps making me feel really good.

Finally, though I am immensely appreciative of compliments in the way of writing prowess and clever insight, any aptitude—mechanical or otherwise—should be properly credited to the grace of God and the working of the Spirit. Left to my own abilities, I am utterly incapable.

The buildings sleep along the river.
The boats wait in shadows.
Movie signs, crossing cops, window tracks
and different colored suits of clothes;
odors, noises, lights
and a mysteriously tender pattern of walls—
these lie in the night like a reward.

We walk away with memories. When we are
traveling some day, riding over strange
places, these will be things we shall
remember.

. . . And we shall sit staring at famous
monuments, battlefields, antiquities, and
whisper to ourselves:
'. . . wish I was back . . . . wish I was back . . .'

—BEN HECHT, 1921

Introduction

Like the earth of a hundred years ago, our mind still has its darkest Africas, its unmapped Borneos and Amazon basins. In relation to the fauna of these regions we are not yet zoologists, we are mere naturalists and collectors of specimens.

. . . [T]he creatures inhabiting these remote regions of the mind are exceedingly improbable. Nevertheless they exist, they are facts of observation; and as such they cannot be ignored by anyone who is honestly trying to understand the world in which he lives.

—Aldous Huxley, *Heaven and Hell*

T HOUGH J.B. RHINE, founder of Duke University's imaginative (if ill-fated) parapsychology lab, gained far more fame than his like-minded wife, Louisa Rhine was herself a tremendous force behind *psi* research. While J.B. labored long and hard in his studies of extrasensory perception, precognition, and clairvoyance, struggling to discover a replicable *psi* effect acceptable to "proper" science, Louisa, with a diligence almost unheard of, collected, year after year and one by one, about 50,000 individual, written accounts of paranormal experience. Her file, composed of countless pages of testimony to psychic phenomena of every kind, remains perhaps the most extensive and extraordinary collection of personal *psi* experience today. Ironically, Louisa's efforts were little heralded by twentieth-century scientists, who chalked up even these legion testimonies to overactive imaginations, coincidence, and lies.

These days, the collecting of *psi* experiences still goes on, and though the search for a replicable effect is more passionate than ever, there also exists a new appreciation for Louisa Rhine's brand of evidence. Increasingly, parapsychologists are becoming aware of the possibility that so-called spontaneous paranormal phenomena are not normal only in their unwillingness to be subject to "normal" science—

that is, the paradigm that rules us right now.

These spontaneous phenomena, the happenings ranging from poltergeists to premonitions, with lots of things in between, are once again being studied as very legitimate experiences, worthy of the efforts of eminently distinguished researchers. Just if and how the study of these phenomena will merge with the tedious attempts at laboratory control of *psi* ability is, like many of the phenomena themselves, still a mystery. While the struggle to tie them together goes on, one can only keep collecting.

The stories in this volume may seem far from the kind of scientific-mindedness for which the Rhines were famous. The accounts are largely entertaining, as they are meant to interpret a city's history and culture from a rather thrilling angle. Some of the stories are likely totally fantastic: the predictable haunting of infamous places like the headquarters of mobsters, the homes of the rich and famous, and the sites of unthinkable and widely affecting disasters. Yet, others are less explicable, and, ironically, more open to scientific scrutiny. They are also more universal: the vision of a soldier crossing a child's bedroom; the sighting of dead woman above her buried ashes; the sound of one's name when no one is near. Psychologists have neatly dismissed a universe of such experiences with the explanation of hallucination—visual ones, auditory ones, even olfactory ones—and our incredible twentieth-century faith in psychology tends to concur.

That is, until we have an experience of our own.

Then, the real-as-can-be nature of it—the person in our house who isn't there at all, the familiar voice of a dead relative calling out our name, the smell of a loved one's perfume long after her passing—reveals hallucination as a poor label indeed.

Since the publication of the first edition of *Chicago Haunts* in the fall of 1997, I have been virtually bombarded with letters, phone calls, and e-mail correspondence from Chicago-area residents eager to share their own experiences with that vast world we call, for sheer lack of knowledge of it, the Unknown. When I conducted the exhausting research for that first volume of tales, I was solidly determined to keep out any of the solitary experiences I'd heard of, those dime-a-dozen stories of Grandma's *post mortem* bedside visit and other such reports, convinced that, in order to present a legitimate portrait of the city's so-called ghostlore, I would have to sift out all the truly personal experiences and include only the safe and oft-repeated legends with which I'd grown up, enthralled.

This book is what I sifted out—and then some.

Resolving to give fair play to the engrossing personal testimonies I'd collected, but neglected, I had planned to gather together this extraordinary batch of solitary supernaturalia into a tiny volume of "true ghost stories," erasing any connection to Chicago itself and treating the experiences as universal phenomena. Yet, as I reopened my file of letters and phone messages and read them through, for the first time all at once, I was utterly struck by the "Chicagoanism" before me. In each letter, each note, however detailed or dashed-off, the Windy City origin of the phantom in question was obvious. The jewelry-snatching spirit of the Slomka family was not a universal resident, but plainly belonged to the South Side neighborhood of Beverly; the phantom soldier spotted by Lee Grossman during the Second World War could not have been comfortable in any but a Hyde Park home; and the haunting of north Campbell Avenue was not the work of some run-of-the-mill loved one, but of Mrs. Carl Wanderer, whose murder was avenged by the peerlessly poison pen of *Chicago Daily News* notable Ben Hecht.

As I turned page after page of carefully-scripted testimonies and sorted through the scraps of hastily-scrawled messages, the provincialism became ever more vivid and ever more wonderful: the mysterious voice in the bushes at Montrose Point's "Magic Hedge"; the ghost of a man waiting eternally for his erstwhile dancing partner in Navy's Pier's pre-renovation ballroom; the shade of a belligerent Bucktown barkeep tormenting his customers after his own suicide; the Boy Scouts chased out of a Northwest Side forest preserve by a throng of unseen camp-crashers. This was not the stuff of a generic ghost log, to be thrown to a national public ravenous for the paranormal. This was, once again, a project for the people: the Chicagoans, North and South, West and, yes, even East—whom I've come to know so gladly in these short but engaging years of discovery, these years in which so many have been so willing to share with me their beliefs and experiences, however bizarre they may have seemed.

This sharing is something I've hoped to make very plain in this volume, and to this end, I've included wherever possible or practical the written or transcribed testimony of a firsthand or—in rare cases—second-hand witness to the extraordinary events involved. For while I have been hailed by some kind souls as a grand storyteller, thanks to *Chicago Haunts*, there is no contest, in my mind, between my rehashing and the real thing: the true encounter as told by the encounterer. I think that, after reading a number of each ahead, you'll agree.

Although I have included the more private of the city's tales in this volume, I have accompanied them with further forays into Chicago's haunted history, studies of the very public and infinitely eerie sites that continue to play a role in Chicago's collective consciousness, both as a city and as a people. Similarly, I have also included supernatural legends tied to those places that, while not technically part of Chicago or its suburbs, play a never-ending role in the Chicago experience—richly storied sites like the Indiana Dunes, Starved Rock State Park, Michigan's Upper Peninsula, and others.

The reader of the tales ahead will find that many of the sites connected to the stories have been drastically altered in the course of time and progress. The sand dunes that hosted the Fort Dearborn Massacre are concrete streets now, the site of the bloodbath itself occupied by an outmoded factory, the neighborhood having gone from windswept to whirlwind and nearly back again to abandonment in the space of less than 200 years, a fact which speaks volumes to the student of urban history. Al Capone's longtime digs at the Lexington Hotel were demolished along with the rest of the building a generation ago, leaving the ubiquitous vacant lot for crime buffs' photo-ops. The so-called "Murder Castle" which towered over the Englewood neighborhood was razed soon after H.H. Holmes was hanged for the torture and death of dozens behind the very doors of that Chicago home; the old Ovaltine factory in Villa Park is metamorphosing into an ultra-chic condominium complex.

Yet, it is for the memory of these places that these books and, really, all ghost stories, exist: when the physical remains of life—great or grim life—are gone, ghosts keep the memory of what we did (and where we did it) alive and well. In this somehow desperate Chicago time of massive gentrification and the resulting displacement of thousands upon thousands of native Chicagoans, this keeping is more crucial than ever. Indeed, it may be all that lasts.

Therefore, seek here and everywhere to reconstruct the days before these hauntings: the rollicking Chicago days of Capone's Prohibition-era South Side, the incredible Chicago days of H.H. Holmes during the thrilling and threatening years of the waning nineteenth century; the carefree days when Ovaltine scented the suburbs with chocolate and answered fan mail addressed to a local orphan named Annie.

Everywhere, seek what Chicago is ever made of.

Not the dead, but the once and boldly alive.

GOLD STAR HAUNTS

Photo by D. Cowan.

This Division Street landmark is the place to be unseen.

In the Company of Strangers
at a West Town Tavern

BY THE TIME THE Division Street institution called the Gold Star Bar was purchased in 1990 by three Chicagoans aiming to make a go at saloon-keeping, the place had seen a varied past. Vintage photos depicting the West Town neighborhood in the early part of the twentieth century capture the sumptuous interior of an ornately-wallpapered and lavishly-furnished pub. And while the post-war years saw a relative decline of the establishment into just another of the legion of gin mills along "Polish Broadway"—so nicknamed for the intense concentration of Poles living here and the bars they opened on literally every corner— the tavern would see its worst times in the 1960s, when female dancers decorated the bar and offered themselves for hire in the rooms upstairs, the ramshackle apartments split between hookers and addicts. In those days, arguments between hard-living local types made bar fights along Division *de rigueur*, and the sparring that ensued here, some of it deadly, made a night on Polish Broadway quite interesting.

Today, the Gold Star occupies that precious space, both cultural and physical, between Bucktown/Wicker Park yuppie life and the old neighborhood world memorialized by local boy Nelson Algren. The go-go dancers and their bedrooms are gone, the three stories of apartments are occupied by regular folks, though the occasional derelict still inquires about a flop now and then. Yet, with a past of such ill repute, it should not surprise that this rather trendy North Side tavern should serve up a few of its own choice spirits.

In addition to the less-than-desirables who frequented the Gold Star in its poorer years, a number of hot-blooded killings are reported to have taken place here over the generations, including the one that occurred in the 1950s, when a previous bartender shot a would-be holdup man in the tavern's front doorway. Susan Stursberg, an employee of the Gold Star for nearly ten years, has long felt a degree of discomfort in this area of the bar, whether opening or closing up for the night or socializing in the vicinity. She has also wondered from time to time about strange movements in her peripheral vision.

Fellow employees back up Stursberg's unease. One bartender, while getting supplies out of a back room, was startled when the room's light went out on its own. Suspecting a problem with the bulb or a fuse, he went to turn off the wall switch—and found that the switch itself had been flipped off by unseen fingers. Similarly, previous tenants of the building's top floor frequently talked about their ghost who turned the TV and stereo on and off periodically.

As for the seeing of ghosts in this place, several have had differing encounters with invisible patrons and residents of the building. An artist living upstairs has drawn sketches of two gender-ambiguous faces he claims to sense in the building. A visiting psychic reported the presence of two female spirits, one old and one younger, claimed to clairvoyantly hear the sound of high heels clicking across the upstairs floors, and pointed to a presence in the bar's front doorway—the site of the murder of a half-century ago.

Ian Tuggle, another longtime Gold Star employee, has even better evidence of otherworldlies here: Tuggle has actually *seen* one of them—and in living color:

> It was the last time the Bulls won the championship, and the bar was really crowded. Everyone was staring at the TVs, and I was running for a million drinks. At one point, I was putting away a lot of bottles—I had my arms full of them—and I looked at the side of me, and I saw someone behind the bar with me, near where we have the control for the jukebox volume. Well, we've had people who think they can come behind the bar and do things like that, and I was going to yell at them. So I turned, and the person I saw was—it was a woman—was wearing this bright green, almost lime green type of dress. And I decided, well, I've got to yell at someone, so I put down the bottles and turned around to face her, and there was absolutely no one there.
>
> Now, this person had been standing practically right next to me and, though I hadn't been looking right at her, it was something I definitely saw. And though she couldn't have gone anywhere

that fast, I still scanned the entire bar, and there was no one in there with that color dress on. And at that point, I turned to Susan, another bartender, and said, *Well, I just saw a ghost.*

The first person to report actually seeing a ghost was a Gold Star regular who came in to shoot pool. He witnessed what seemed to be a "normal" man, except that he was wearing suspenders and a banded straw hat, disappear upon walking to the bathroom. There one minute, gone the next.

While no one has tried to specifically identify the seemingly numerous spirits here at the Gold Star, an air of sadness does seem to flavor the accounts of those who've encountered them. The artist who has drawn them illustrates a genuine melancholia on at least one face, and the psychic who made the rounds of the building declared an overpowering despair. After touring the basement of the storied structure, the sensitive felt an almost audible despondence.

Said she: *It was as if the very walls were crying.*

Susan Stursberg and Ian Tuggle shared their accounts of the Gold Star Bar with the author in telephone interviews conducted in the summer of 2000.

LUETGERT HAUNTS

Author's photo.

Adolph Luetgert's Hermitage Avenue is no more.
The street where his factory once stood is destined to
be the common driveway of these "exciting" new homes.

Meat Meets Murder
as the Century Turns

WHEN, IN 1897, CHICAGO sausage mogul Adolph Luetgert was convicted of murdering his wife, Louisa, and sentenced to life imprisonment at Joliet State Penitentiary, the word on the streets was that Louisa's scheming husband had, according to an evil children's rhyme, "made sausage out of his wife."

Adolph's methods weren't quite as extreme, however, as the city's nose-diving sausage sales suggested. Louisa did enter her husband's sausage factory in one piece on the night of May 1, 1897, never to be seen whole again. But the job Adolph did on his bride was a private affair, discovered by determined detectives—not unsuspecting diners.

That spring before Louisa's disappearance, heated arguments had for months cut through the neighborhood surrounding the Luetgert house, near Hermitage and Diversey Avenues. Brash and unembarrassed, the words between the Luetgerts made clear the couple's trouble: Louisa's niece, Mary Siemering, had come to work for the Luetgerts as a housekeeper. Demure and darling, she had captured the fancy of the man of the house, and Louisa was on to their trysts. Friends and relatives of Louisa were alarmed then when one morning Louisa was simply gone. She had, without notice, decided to take a trip to visit an aunt in Kenosha. Or so Adolph explained.

Wasting little time, friends of the absentee housewife besieged police, laying their unease on the table, backing up their fear with frank tales of the Luetgerts' marriage woes. Well aware of the couple's instability, the law latched on.

Gaining access to Adolph's sausage works, detectives soon discovered two gold rings in a 12-foot-long potash vat, one of them inscribed with the initials L.L. Fragments of a human skull were tediously removed from the smokestack, from which an anonymous witness had seen smoke pouring on the night of Louisa's disappearance, even though the factory had been closed for some two months due to reorganization. Circumstantial evidence piled high enough to suffocate Adolph Luetgert, who was arrested within the week and taken to a holding cell in the east Chicago Avenue police station to await trial.

No witnesses testified to Luetgert's guilt; still, the rings, the unidentified but obvious remains, and the ready tools of death in the shape of meat saws, furnaces, and boiling vats convinced all but one jury member of Adolph's evil deed. The jury was dismissed and Luetgert was retried a second time. The has-been meatmaker was convicted of murder and sentenced to life imprisonment, despite the fact that Louisa's body had never been found.

Adolph Luetgart spent a scant two years in prison, but what years they were. From his cell far south of his old factory, he wailed through the days and nights, crying for release, claiming his innocence. Inmates believed in Luetgert's guilt, convinced that Louisa's spirit was incarcerated with him—taunting him, terrorizing him. Relatives and other visitors who witnessed Luetgert's scenes became convinced of the truth of this tale—but not Adolph's defense attorney, Lawrence Harmon. Harmon was determined to prove that Luetgert was innocent of his wife's murder; to this end, he spent thousands of dollars of his own savings in his personal hunt for the "lost" Louisa. Ultimately, he entered an insane asylum. Luetgert himself died at the turn of the century, haunted to death, they say, by his vengeful wife.

After Adolph's passing, rumors arose that Louisa's ghost had returned to the couple's home adjoining the sausage factory on Chicago's North Side. There, the new owner would catch frequent glimpses of her standing by the mantel in the parlor. Legend says that he was so annoyed with this pesky boarder that he actually had the house removed from the site, relocating it to a lot on Marshfield Avenue. After the house was gone, Louisa began appearing to security guards in the old sausage factory next door, where she would wander between the basement incinerator and the vat where her rings had been found by police. When, in 1902, the factory burned down in a freak fire, Louisa actually moved again—this time back to her old house, now on Marshfield. Frustrated by the phantom's return, the owner sought to placate Louisa by moving the building a second time, back near its original spot at Diversey and Hermitage, in order to give the ghost some peace and, hopefully, get rid of her for good.

She's still there.

The author was alerted to the Luetgert hauntings by Dylan Clearfield's Chicagoland Ghosts. *An engaging account of the murder itself can be found in Richard Lindberg's* Return to the Scene of the Crime.

BLUEBERRY HOUSE HAUNTS

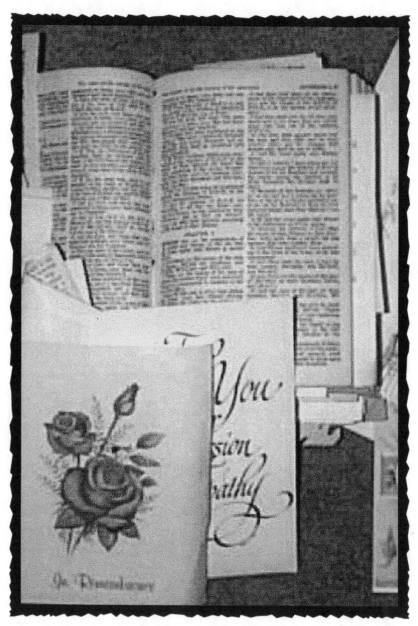

Witness's photo.

Cards and letters from this Bible find their way into
surprising places in a southwest suburban home.

A Dreadfully Delicious Ghost Story

MANY MISTAKENLY BELIEVE THAT hauntings are hallmarked by visual apparitions alone and, clearly, the seeing of ghosts has been the traditional sign of lingering spirits. Yet, most phantoms choose to show themselves not with full-form figures but by appealing to our other senses. In fact, visual apparitions are the rarest of all; most disembodied types confront us in the form of sensations, sounds, and even smells.

Midlothian resident Lori Warner* is a rare and ongoing witness to a curious but common type of *psi* phenomenon: the olfactory apparition; that is, the scent of something that isn't there. Her longtime home in Chicago's far southwest suburbs hosts a deceptively delicious, altogether unwarranted aroma. This smell, along with an array of inexplicable phenomena, does a nice job of haunting the Warner house:

> Certainly one of the oldest houses on the block, the big blue house on Central Park is anything but imposing. Standing two stoies tall, it has a quiet, farmhouse-like charm about it. During the Second World War the house was divided into two complete living quarters, one on each floor. The upstairs area was made into a one-bedroom apartment and the downstairs became a two-bedroom apartment. From that point on, the house became rental property and passed through a few hands before we found it. The house was offered to us through a friend who was currently living in it. She had been renting the downstairs apartment and had an opportunity to rent the house next door. We were overjoyed, as we had been living in an apartment building and my husband and I were looking for a place with a yard and a garage.
>
> The first few weeks in the house were uneventful. But one afternoon I was sitting in the living room watching TV and the chan-

nels started changing. Thinking that I was sitting on the remote, I got up and checked. I looked under the cushions of the couch and found nothing. I eventually located the remote sitting on an end table. It obviously had nothing to do with the channels changing. I picked it up and hit the power button. The television clicked off and then suddenly clicked on again. I tried to shut it off with the power button on the TV and the same thing happened. By this time, all the hairs on my arms and legs were standing on end. About the time that I had decided to pull the plug on the machine, the channel switching had stopped and everything went back to normal. I recounted this episode to the daughter of the previous tenant (who now lived next door) and she told me that this sort of thing had happened all the time to her in the house. She also asked me not to tell her mother about it because her mother viewed this type of thing as "pure nonsense." Obviously, her mother had been spared the experience herself. The television incidents continued for a while and evolved into other, more frightening phenomena.

It usually began in the early morning hours, about one or two o'clock. I would wake up suddenly and, for some reason, I would be afraid. I attributed this feeling to the possibility of just having woken up from a bad dream, although I could not remember any. There is a nineteen-inch television set at the end of my bed, sitting on a chest of drawers. I looked up at the set, and it was glowing.

I called to my husband, Tony*, who was sleeping in the living room on the couch because he was having back trouble. When I got a conscious response from him, I asked him if he had ever seen a television set glow. He told me that they sometimes retain an aura after they had been recently turned off. I reminded him that I had been sleeping for several hours and the set had been off since ten o'clock. He told me to check and see if any light was coming from the window that the TV might have picked up. I did. The blinds were completely closed; not a single ray of light was coming through them. At this point, the light on the screen began to fade and the set returned to a normal state. I rationalized that there might be some quirk that I could attribute to this particular brand of TV, and we switched the set with a newer one that had been in the basement. Since that first night, this has happened many more times. Always in the early morning, with the newer set. I have never seen any other set in any other room do this. Tony ignores it now, and I put my head under the covers and wait for it to go away. The terrified feeling always precedes the event.

Another frightening incident occurred in the living room, within this same period. My husband and I were sitting and watching TV one afternoon. My cat was sitting on the couch next to me. I had been petting her on and off as I watched the program. Suddenly I saw the cat jump up on the entertainment center, get tangled in the lamp cord, and pull the lamp to the ground. When I yelled to my husband, *stop the cat*, he only looked at me in horror and pointed to the cat still sitting by my side. She, too, was staring at the empty space where the lamp had been. We searched for the animal that had caused the disturbance. I swore that I had seen a cat. My husband, grasping for an explanation, suggested a mouse.

Some mouse. The cause, to this day, remains a mystery.

I learned later, from older neighbors, that the original owners of the house had been dog breeders. They had raised small dogs, chihuahuas and dachshunds. Several doors in the basement of the house had been cut in half, similar to a barn door, and supported the dog-breeding story. Also in the basement, next to the furnace, was an incinerator. A similar incinerator was located in a shed to the rear of the property. We can only speculate as to the purpose they served. An aunt of mine suggested that they might have been used to burn waste material, such as bedding from the dogs. My children as well as my sister had often reported to me that they felt uneasiness in the basement area of the house. Whenever my sister would go downstairs to do her laundry, she insisted that she kept seeing things out of the corners of her eyes. When she turned to look, they were gone. She described what she saw as "kind of like small animals." At this time, we had no knowledge of the dogs that had been raised there.

Although these incidents had truly frightened me, the next occurrence had a much milder effect and became a fairly common feature of the house. The family and I would return from shopping or visiting to find the house completely filled with the fresh-baked smell of blueberry pies or muffins. We questioned the tenant upstairs, who also smelled "the pies cooking" but could offer no explanation as to where the scent was coming from. We checked outside, too, and found no aroma there. It seemed as if the smells were coming right out of the heat ducts and filling the house. They were not unpleasant and, of course, produced a strong craving for freshly-baked pie. Eventually, we purchased the house, despite this phenomenon, which continued for several years. Believe it or not, we would actually "fall" for the mysterious baking smell over and over again. We would get excited, run upstairs, and ask my sister (who was now renting the apartment) where the muffins were. By this time she would laugh and ask us when we were ever going to learn.

After my sister moved on, we turned the house into a single-family dwelling using the upstairs as bedrooms. The baking aromas stopped suddenly with the removal of the oven from the upstairs apartment and the disposal of a large freezer from the basement.

Further incidents in the house have involved missing and replaced articles, or items appearing from "out of the blue." Several days before my brother's anniversary, I was mopping the kitchen floor. The floor had been swept before washing, and I left for a moment to fill a bucket from the tub. When I returned, I saw— directly in the middle of the room—what looked to be a card. I went and picked it up, only to discover that it was an invitation to my brother's wedding two years earlier. In three days, it would be the anniversary date. I had always kept these cards in a box in the basement, yet I didn't think much of it. I was, in fact, grateful, as I had time to send a card to the couple. I became more surprised as this began to happen more frequently, with the cards appearing more often, just days before the events. The most recent occurred just days before this writing. My husband came in from work with a memorial card in his hand. The card was from the funeral of a friend who had died tragically in a motorcycle accident several years ago. Tony had found the card on the passenger seat of his work truck.

The anniversary of the death would be in two days.

Alternate names have been used at the request of the eyewitness, who shared her story of the Blueberry Ghost with the author in a written account during the summer of 2000.

AL CAPONE HAUNTS

Photo courtesy of Richard Lindberg.

The ghost of Al Capone was said to saunter from window to window
at the old Lexington Hotel, pictured here before its demolition.

Never Give up the Ship

ALPHONSE **CAPONE LEFT LONG** shadows on the city he owned. Some say that, in light of continuing corruption at City Hall and the shady dealings of police brass, Capone still owns Chicago more than half a century after his decidedly inglorious death. Haunted in their own way by the villain's indestructible and international image, recent administrations have led aggressive but covert campaigns to eradicate from the city's face all traces of Capone's kingdom. To the chagrin of crime buffs, Chicago razed, one by one, the accidental memorials to the town's gangland glory, from the Four Deuces Saloon where the Brooklyn boy got his Chi-town start to the garage where he waged the battle that won his war: the S-M-C Cartage Company garage on north Clark Street, where Capone's men carried out the St. Valentine's Day Massacre of 1929.

As any ghosthunter knows, the site of that old garage, now the parking lot of a Chicago Housing Authority hi-rise, still rings with the screams of that freezing Chicago day so long ago. Posh Lincoln Parkers wince as they pass, troubled by the insistent wails that seem to have no source. Others, walking their dogs, are puzzled by the animals' fear of the lot; unfamiliar with the history of the place, they drag their pets past it, annoyed by their frantic barking and whimpering.

But Capone is not here.

Far northwest of the city, all over Elgin and other towns along the winding path of the Fox River, roadhouses and residences tucked into seclusion tell tales of Capone. These are towns full of houses said to be haunted by prostitutes, gamblers, and rum-runners who turned up on the wrong side of Capone . . . and the wrong side of the grave. Houses said to be haunted by Capone himself (who apparently slept in as many Illinois beds as Abraham Lincoln).

But Capone is not here.

In life, Capone stayed always at the center of the action, most notably at the old Lexington Hotel south of Chicago's Loop. From his suite on an upper floor, he ran Chicago and ruined lives. Though he died in his Florida home, where he'd been when he'd "heard" of the St. Valentine's Day Massacre, it was here that he should have returned to spend his eternity. And he did, at least for a while. From the time of his death until the demolition of the building in the 1990s, passers-by on south Michigan Avenue often spotted a glimmering form moving from room to room in the windows of the abandoned hotel. When talk arose of the landmark's razing, more than a few natives, convinced of Al's presence at the place, wondered where Capone would go. Though some modern-day fans hoped he would resurface elsewhere in Chicago, most prayed for a speedy trip, Heaven- or Hell-ward, for the hoodlum, tired of the sordid Chicago his memory continued to foster.

Fans rejoice.

Soon after the destruction of the Lexington, the owners of Capone's old pleasure boat, *Duchess III*, experienced a lively new flurry of supernaturalism on the already haunted yacht. Those familiar with the craft's history wondered at the activity: had the boat's erstwhile captain returned to the only helm he had left?

During his reign, Al Capone spent his off-hours indulging in luxurious leisure, hunting and fishing with often great success. The *Duchess III*, named after a particularly enchanting prostitute in Al's employ, was only one in a collection of cruisers that Capone kept up. After a decade of use, the pristine craft gradually deteriorated. When new owners began a tedious restoration of the darkly historic *Duchess*, they discovered a few extra hands on board: the yacht was definitely haunted. In fact, so frequent are the visual and audio apparitions in one below-deck area, it has been christened the "ghost room." The owners and their guests have heard a baby's wails and a woman's cries and have even viewed a phantom replay of a tempestuous scene: a male figure grabbing a baby from a woman's arms and throwing the child overboard.

Along with the troubling spectres, a number of individuals have confronted intense "cold spots" on board the *Duchess*: freezing pockets of air that paralyze the body, even in sweltering heat.

Even from the shore, the ship confounds. Time and again, local fishermen have watched a flame-like light moving among the portholes of the *Duchess* when she was supposedly deserted.

Capone himself was no stranger to the supernatural. Fifteen years before his death, he contacted psychic Alice Britt, pleading for her help in ridding him of a very personal phantom: the ghost of St. Valentine's Day Massacre victim, and Bugs Moran's brother-in-law, James Clark, who Capone claimed had been harassing him since Clark's brutal death.

For nearly 20 years, friends and bodyguards witnessed the disturbing interplay between Al and his unseen oppressor. Day and night Capone's weeping could be heard, punctuated by mad begging to be left alone. Sympathetic skeptics reason that the syphilis Al battled in his later years caused his insanity. Surely, they say, this is the source of the "ghost" he imagined: Capone's own guilt made monstrous by disease-inspired hallucinations.

But if this is true, Capone certainly would have been mad, the guilt of the hundreds of deaths he commissioned peopling his mind with an army of apparitions. James Clark was, then, only a representative illusion—or very real indeed.

The author is indebted to a number of anonymous individuals for their personal accounts of the Duchess *haunting. An entertaining and detailed record of the haunting of Al Capone, and his yacht, appears in Dylan Clearfield's* Chicagoland Ghosts, *which will delight fans and foes of Chicago's original boss.*

BEVERLY HILLS HAUNTS

Home Remodeling Rip-Offs

Tales of foiled renovations abound in the annals of *psi* experience. Frustratingly common are the stories of young couples who move into frumpy but fabulous old homes ready and willing to put all their time, money, and effort into restoring them to their original glory, only to have new floorboards pried up by unseen hands, tools stolen by invisible thieves, and fresh paint smeared by ghostly fingers. Despite the good intentions of the new owners, previous residents (perhaps unconvinced of their own departure) are unwilling to let a troupe of trespassers fiddle with their private homes. Others, less stubborn, are content to merely oversee the operations, either silently or with a few unobtrusive but attention-getting moves.

The Beverly Hills neighborhood of Chicago's far South Side is rife with such untold tales. Best known for the long and varied haunting of the so-called Irish Castle, the home built by Charles Givens in a curious architectural style, now housing the Beverly Unitarian Church, Beverly is also home to some unsung haunts; namely, the frenzy of phantoms that inhabit the area's stately old residences, many of them under renovation.

When, in 1974, the Slomka family moved into their century-old house, they, like so many of the city's purchasers, were greeted with the prospect of endless work. Ahead of them lay months of restoration: time and effort made worthwhile by the gorgeous oak staircase, built-in leaded-glass china cabinets, and ornate fireplaces. The residence had been occupied by one family since 1917; after 60 years in the house, the last of the family died in the house. Though the previous owners had done what remodeling they could manage, the house was, in Gloria Slomka's words, "a mess, to put it mildly."

In the weeks before the work began, the Slomkas lived in the house "as-is," holding the peeling plaster and crumbling walls at bay with dreams of what would be after their project was complete. During that time, the quiet of the noble neighborhood prevailed in the house, which seemed silently suspended in another era. Then, soon after the renovations began, an unexpected development shed a whole new light on the restoration: the Slomkas realized that, despite the deed in their hands, one of the house's old owners had somehow remained, overseeing the changes, and the new family. Gloria Slomka remembers the revelation and the incredible events that followed:

> I was expecting our fifth child in April. We had moved in the previous November, and I was not prepared for the amount of work we would have to do to restore the house. I don't know what we were thinking when we looked at it. . . .
>
> My husband is an architect, and he set about remodeling the house, starting in the sun parlor. At that time we started to hear strange noises at night, like someone wandering around the house. At first I thought it was just old house noises. But they became louder and they would wake the kids sometimes. We did choose to try to ignore them, as they were not hurting anything.
>
> And then Stephen was born.
>
> The baby was just a few days old and sleeping in his bassinet in our bedroom. I got up in the middle of the night and walked over to check him, and as I bent down, there was this overwhelming smell of roses all around him.
>
> After that experience, we never heard the strange noises again.
>
> Though the sounds stopped, the presence was still very much with us. She, whoever she was, made herself known in other ways. She would take pieces of jewelry and keep them for a while. When I'd misplace them, the girls and I would search for the missing pieces in all the drawers, across the floors and in all of my pockets. After we had gone over every possible place, the pieces would always turn up in a place where we had looked, just sitting there very obvious.
>
> Sometimes, if you asked her to give them back, she would.

The events chronicled in this account were extracted from a written testimony by Gloria Slomka, composed for the author in the spring of 2000.

WRIGLEY FIELD HAUNTS

Author's photo.

Under Michigan Avenue, the Billy Goat glimmers.
Across town, the hometown favorites flounder.

Hexes, Harmonies,
... and Harry

STEP OUT OF THE rat-riddled gloom of lower Michigan Avenue and have a couple. Down here, in the Billy Goat Tavern, all is bright and beautiful.

Ghosts are the last thing on the minds of the Billy Goat's loyal and loquacious patrons, these mostly jaded journalists swaying on the stools far beneath the Sun-Times building and the Tribune Tower. Of course, the dead and buried are always here, notably Mike Royko and cheezborger-loving John Belushi, both of whom did their best to make the Goat immortal, on the tips of the tongues of those who loved them. True phantoms, however, would be out of place in the Billy Goat, and so they take their business elsewhere, it seems.

What does live on in the Billy Goat is talk, which, though not on the menu, is dirt cheap and always on tap. Talk about the news, talk about the town, talk about the weather, and, in this Near North dram shop, always, always talk about the Cubs. And, weirdly enough, it was the Cubs that led the Billy Goat into dealings with the Other Side.

This is a once-upon-a-time tale.

Once upon a time, the Chicago Cubs were playing in the World Series. For sticklers, it was 1945. As a publicity stunt, William "Billy Goat" Sianis, owner of the Billy Goat Tavern, attempted to bring his "pet" goat with him into Wrigley Field. When entry was refused to the goat, Sianis placed a curse on the team. The rest, of course, is baseball history.

The Curse of the Cubs has served as a fine . . . well, *scapegoat* for the team's disastrous non-World Series seasons—the last 55 of them, to be exact. Though blamed summer after summer, some years the possibility of a curse seemed almost reasonable: in 1984 San Diego, for example, when the ball rolled through Leon Durham's legs in Game 5 of the National League Championship Series.

Fun is fun, however, and after decades of hometown humiliation, current Billy Goat owner Sam Sianis attempted to lift the Cubs curse: once on *The Tonight Show with Jay Leno* and once by walking a goat around Wrigley during the 13th home game of the season, after the Cubs had lost 12 home games in a row. When the Cubs beat the Reds that day, hopes for the team's salvation flew higher than the balls onto Waveland Avenue, but alas, the Unknown was only teasing. In 1997, Cub fans marveled at just how bad things had become, as they endured game after game of the worst losing streak in the team's 121-year history.

That year, after weeks of straight losses and waning allegiance on the part of even the most die-hard of the Cubs' famously loyal fans, a sign went up in one of Wrigleyville's apartment windows: *Put the goat in*, it said.

Indeed.

These days, Wrigley Field is haunted by more than curses.

After the death, in the late 1990s, of Harry Caray, longtime and beloved Cubs announcer, a team of paranormal investigators scanned Wrigley Field for evidence that Caray had lingered. The reason? A curious, and downright uncomfortable, winning streak that threatened to bring the Cubs to the threshold of the Series. As our unusually well-playing club ran the bases, fans whispered about a guardian Harry, tapping his newfound powers to lead his Cubbies to victory.

Not so fast.

Loyal to their loser image, the Cubs ultimately fizzled. Nonetheless, that early autumn investigation bore some strange fruit: the discovery by ghosthunters of a spot in the bleachers alive with electromagnetic energy, directly across the ball field from Caray's old seat. Was this evidence of a phantom Harry, his ghostly eyes boring an ethereal hole across his sightline and into the stands? Perhaps, though no unusual energies were at play in the announcer's box itself. Perhaps, instead, the mysterious presence in the bleachers can be credited to one of Wrigley's finer bums—musician Steve Goodman, who wrote the team's unofficial anthem, "Go,Cubs, Go," and "A Dying Cub Fan's Last Request."

Tied to the ballpark by a lifetime of affection, the dying Goodman couldn't bear the thought of leaving his team. For his loyalty, he was granted his own last request: a box-seat ticket to every Cubs game to come.

Goodman's ashes are buried here at Wrigley Field—his loyal fingers figuratively crossed forever—right under home plate.

Octavia Avenue Haunts

Author's photo.

Near this sleepy Northwest Side intersection,
a remarkable neighbor holds her ground.

Home Again

T HE HOUSE IN THE 5400 block of north Octavia was no stranger to bizarre phenomena. When Barbara Kroner was a girl there, the doorbell began ringing wildly at the moment her grandmother died. Though the family was seated in the living room in full view of the front door, no one could be seen outside, frantically trying to enter the unlocked house. Still, the bell just kept ringing.

When Barbara's father, Hubert Nelsen, bought his wife, Frances, the lovely dwelling on Chicago's Northwest Side, she instantly fell in love with the place. Everything about it seemed like home. Frances had, in her younger days, worked as a model for the old Boston Store in the Loop; the "homey" character she displayed after moving into the house was utterly alien to those familiar with her sleek, urban sophistication. When they observed her at work in her new home, however, the source of the change was evident: she just loved that house.

Frances wanted to be home all the time; parties, outings, shopping—all the trappings of a young model's life—paled in comparison to the dreamy hours spent working in the garden or preparing the family's meals in her cozy kitchen.

Despite her joys, illness crept in, and Frances gradually found herself suffering from headaches and other maladies. When her husband, a furniture salesman for Marshall Field & Co., suffered a heart attack, Frances, fearing his death, tried to take her own life first, overdosing on pills in the locked bathroom. When her son and daughter crashed the door in time to save their mother, she was unquestionably irked.

Frances's cheer returned with her husband's unexpected recovery, but only briefly. Forced to move in with their children, the couple sold the house on Octavia, and Frances was devastated. So acute was her grief at the loss, her husband agreed to buy it back. Sadly, just ten months after the move back in, Frances died of her own heart attack at the kitchen table.

According to her wishes, Hubert had his wife cremated and kept her ashes in the living room of the house. When, several years after the death, he married his childhood sweetheart, Hubert decided to have his first wife's ashes buried in a cemetery plot he had purchased for the family. Setting out for the burial, daughter Barbara volunteered to join him on the trip to the cemetery, but Hubert declined her offer, reasoning that an aunt was going with him and that Barbara's going would be an unnecessary trial. Though she insisted on going along, her father was adamantly against it, so at last she agreed and stayed behind.

Several years passed, and both Hubert and his new wife died. After her father's cremation, Barbara decided to bury his ashes alongside her mother's. Contacting the cemetery where the family lots were, she asked to have her father's ashes deposited near her mother's. The silence on the phone was troubling. After several double-checks and more uncomfortable silences, Barbara was told that her mother's ashes were not there.

Stupefied and concerned, Barbara called her step-sister, hoping for some help in locating the missing ashes. *Didn't you know?* asked her step-sister, *Your dad buried your mom's ashes in the backyard of your old house.*

Barbara was dumbstruck and overcome with anxiety. Since her father's death, the house had been sold. The new family, an immigrant woman from Eastern Europe and her mother and son, had moved into the old family home and were well settled in. There was no easy way back to her mother's ashes.

In a panic, Barbara called an old Octavia neighbor to explain the problem. *Don't worry*, she was told. *This new owner is very nice. I'll tell her to call you.*

When, several days later, Barbara received the call from the house's new owner, little did she know what bigger shocks lay in store after the recent ones. When the friendly, gentle voice on the other end asked what the problem was, Barbara explained what she had discovered, expecting rage at worst, disgust at best. What she got, instead, was a remarkable answer.

I just found out that my mother's ashes are buried in your backyard,

Barbara told her.

Well, we sort of already knew that, the new owner replied.

How can that be? I didn't even know, wondered Barbara.

And the simple explanation: *Because we've seen her out there.*

There had been times, the new owner said, since they'd moved in, that she'd watched a blonde woman in a long dress, throwing a ball for the dog out in the backyard. She wasn't the only one to see her. Her son and her mother had seen her, too.

Barbara remembers that when she heard this she fell backwards into a chair, overwhelmed. As a girl in that house, Barbara had owned a precious dog. Even more taken with the dog than Barbara was her mother. When the dog underwent painful surgery for a medical problem, Barbara's mother would crawl under the table and spoon-feed the dog until it had regained its strength. For years, the two spent long, happy hours out back, Frances standing under a favorite peach tree given to her by her mother-in-law, throwing a ball for the dog to fetch. When Barbara married, her mother said, *You go ahead and get married, but the dog stays with me. He'll be here whenever you want to see him.* When the pet eventually died, Frances insisted on burying it under the tree where they'd played, so that the dog could always be near.

As staggering as the new owner's news was, the problem of the ashes remained. The house's new tenant, however, didn't see any problem, explaining to Barbara that such events tended to be quite common in her native country, that Barbara's mom should stay put. *She's so happy when we see her, and she doesn't bother us at all,* the woman reasoned, *Leave her where she is.*

Barbara left her mother where her father buried her, in the backyard of the house on Octavia. As of this writing, she is still seen there by the new owners, framed by the shamrock-carved garage door she loved, playing an endless game of fetch with her old pal under her favorite tree.

Barbara Kroner gave an oral account of her Octavia Avenue experiences to the author in a telephone interview conducted in the summer of 2000.

INDEPENDENCE GROVE HAUNTS

Author's photo.

Construction at the soon-to-be-dedicated Independence Grove
Forest Preserve: A new face is fitted to an old, old tale.

Unlocking "The Gate"

IN THE SUMMER OF 1999, five Lake County teenagers disappeared into the woods of the Independence Grove Forest Preserve in unincorporated Lake County, Illinois.

They were all seen again.

Not so with the three protagonists featured in 1999's blockbuster "mockumentary," *The Blair Witch Project*, in which three film students traipse off into the forests of Maryland and disappear without a trace. In the community of Burkittsville, where the movie is set, townies were besieged by *Blair Witch* fans in the months after the film's release, all hoping to get the scoop on some real-life horror behind the movie's story line. That mostly ad-libbed screenplay "follows" on a journey of three suburban college students intent on creating a visual history of a grisly legend connected to the old town of Blair, now Burkittsville. After interviewing locals who vaguely describe the chilling abduction and murder of a number of area children in the 1940s by a crazed recluse living in the woods outside Burkittsville, the filmmakers head out to the forest themselves to find and film the sites connected to the story. Central to the legend is the evil spirit of an old woman, the Blair Witch, said to dwell in the woods who, in fact, drove the recluse to his terrible deeds. Ignorant of both the vastness of the Maryland wilderness and the reality of the Blair Witch, the trio leave their car by the roadside and set out into the trees.

As the students record their days and nights in the forest, long, aimless days interrupted by hints of some unknown horror, they gradually become aware that they are lost. As the camera rolls, we are one with these students as the self-assuredness of the modern American suburban mindset gives way to the reality that one can still get lost in America, and that the woods outside the old town of Blair are a bad place to have that happen.

Many viewers of *The Blair Witch Project* were so perplexed by the film that they swore off hiking, camping, and even bike rides through forest preserves, haunted by the "lost" feeling the movie provided. Others delighted in the sensation, like those who made the bizarre pilgrimage to Burkittsville to grill the locals and get lost in the real-life woods there. Still others, electrified by the film, refocused their interest on very local legends, going to nearby woods in search of their own witches.

In and around Chicago, the forest preserves exercise a compelling power over teenagers, drawing them into the little bit of mystery they offer to those weary of city life. In and out of the city, the preserves have overwhelmingly sheltered not only native flora and fauna, but folktales as well. Southwest Siders have long told of the old caretaker of Bachelors Grove Cemetery who went crazy one night and butchered his family after voices in the burial ground told him to do it. Now, his insane spirit roams the Rubio Woods Forest Preserve, including Bachelors Grove Woods and their famous boneyard. North Side kids whisper about Robinson Woods, haunted by early Chicagoan Alexander Robinson, also known as Chief Che-Che-Pin-Quay, whose family phantoms are said to linger around their common gravestone at the edge of the preserve; and about eerie LaBagh Woods, whose groves are rumored to echo with the chant of ghosts. Lately, however, old and new eyes have turned to a familiar site northwest of the city proper: Independence Grove Forest Preserve in unincorporated Lake County.

The site, long a popular one for trespassers in search of kicks, has enjoyed renewed popularity since the 1999 release of *The Blair Witch Project*. The story behind Independence Grove is a chilling one, bearing some ghastly similarities to the *Witch* tale. Most notably, these woods are said to contain some left-behind reminders of a nightmare that went on here some years ago. Local lion hearts, finding extra bravery in numbers, have turned again to the Grove, searching for the truth behind the tale they've heard since childhood.

It *is* a terrible tale.

Years ago, it goes, Independence Grove Forest Preserve was not a preserve at all. Rather, the natural expanse was the sprawling campus of St. Francis School for Girls, a private, exclusive academy in a postcard-perfect setting. All was well and happy at St. Francis, until the gruesome days when a lunatic crept through the trees, stole into the school, and, one by one, abducted a dozen or more of its students. Frantic over the disappearances, police and parents searched the forest day and night in vain in hopes of finding the girls alive. Then, one morning, the sun rose on an appalling sight: the heads of the missing girls, impaled on the spikes of the school gate that still stands on the preserve property today.

Though the killer was caught and, presumably, imprisoned or executed, the trauma shattered the school, which was at once closed and which stood empty for years in the clearing beyond the trees. After talk of a "haunted" school and memories the old building recalled became unbearable to residents and officials, a movement was begun to tear down the school and turn the area into a nature preserve.

This push for the preserve was a great success, and soon, it seemed, all traces of St. Francis School for Girls were gone from the site. The new preserve was christened "Independence Grove" as a tribute to the survivors of the massacre who, through the demolition of the school, had been freed from the physical reminders of that awful night. The event itself was erased from the history books, and locals never looked back, denying the truth of the story to their children who inevitably heard of the tragedy bit by bit when growing up in the northern suburbs.

Though misled for years, local teenagers have gradually pieced the story together, and it is to prove to themselves the truth of the tale that they have, under cover of darkness, repeatedly ventured into Independence Grove. What do they expect to find?

Curiously enough, these kids search for—and reportedly find—again and again, mementos of some sort of school. A rusted locker here, a tattered textbook there. These sinister souvenirs are all it takes to convince them of the reality of the so-called fable of "The Gate," a tale older than most of the houses in these suburbs. Yet, sometimes there is more to bear witness: a trailside whisper that follows close behind, the ring of laughter in an open field, a line of delicate footprints that suddenly ends. Like *The Blair Witch Project*, the tangible evidence joins the ghostly examples to offer quite a compelling story line. There are plenty of takers, despite the risks.

Last summer, five Lake County teenagers attended a showing of *The Blair Witch Project* and, days later, made the news when they received $75 tickets for being in Independence Grove after hours—worth it, they all agreed, for the chance to learn the truth behind "The Gate." *And just what truth did they find?* asked one reporter.

Enough, they responded mysteriously, *to justify the fines.*

David Southwell reported the story of the Lake County teens fined for trespassing at Independence Grove Forest Preserve in a summer 1999 *Chicago Sun-Times* article: "Teens' witch hunt just a ghost story."

NAVY PIER HAUNTS

Photo by D. Bielski.

Pleasure boats round the tip of Navy Pier, crowned
by the curving panes of its restored Grand Ballroom.

A Long Wait for
the Light Fantastic

CHICAGO'S "NEW" LAKEFRONT HAS become the jewel in the crown of Mayor Richard M. Daley, whose push for the City Beautiful has led to a massive overhaul of Chicago's streets and parks, the restoration of its grand boulevards, and the planting of many concrete medians with native trees, shrubs, and flowers. Central to Daley's vision is the reestablishment of the "threshold" Chicago: the rehabilitation, in particular, of the magnificent monuments at Congress Parkway and Michigan Avenue (originally planned as the gateway to the city), the unification of the lakefront museums—The Field Museum of Natural History, the Shedd Aquarium, and the Adler Planetarium—into an easily accessible "museum campus," and, perhaps most notably, the total renovation of Chicago's landmark maritime hub: the Port of Chicago Navy Pier.

The plan to retake Navy Pier for the people was born of decades of disuse, when only a handful of natives strolled the empty lakeside sidewalks for relief from the tourist-clogged arteries of the Streeterville neighborhood and the Loop. Old men and poor men fished near the locks just south of the pier, where a few savvy businessmen came on fine summer days for greasy bags of fried shrimp bought from a clapboard shack.

Philip Wizenick, a security guard on the night watch during those quiet years, remembers the isolated feeling of the old Navy Pier, when the infamous winds whistled through abandoned storage buildings that stretched a half-mile down the center of the pier, ending with a flourish in the crumbling Grand Ballroom at the pier's point, a rusty souvenir of a more elegant age:

During the 1970s, I was working with the Chicago Police Department Port Security Detail at the Port of Chicago Navy Pier. At that time, Navy Pier was a functioning seaport, via the St. Lawrence Seaway, and was jointly operated by North Pier Terminal Warehouse and Great Lakes Terminal and Storage Companies. The building was administered by the department of the Port of Chicago, which also operated the Chicago River bridges and, with the exception of the observation deck above the transit sheds and an occasional trade show or folk festival in the second floor exhibition space, had been closed to the general public. This was especially true of the former entertainment complex at the end of the pier. Prior to World War II, streetcars had run down the center roadway of the pier to the Grand Ballroom. With the onset of conflict, the U.S. Navy turned the pier into an aviation mechanics school. After the War, the University of Illinois at Chicago took over the space, including the north-side ground floor.

The former ballroom with the high, domed roof had been used by UIC as a gym. When the school vacated the pier, bound for Circle Campus, the heat was turned off out there, and Chicago winters took their toll. By 1974, it was in sad shape. The copper roof was leaking, and large portions of the cork ceiling had fallen to the floor. Bricks were popping loose from the walls, windows broken, weeds growing in cracks: a real mess. Also, we had been using the room for target practice, firing at objects placed on the stage—the rear wall of which was full of bullets—and the floor of the auditorium was littered with empty .38 special cartridge cases! To walk across that floor, you had to constantly kick debris and trash out of your way. It was a far cry from the polished dance floor that would be installed a few years later when the buildings at the end of the pier were repaired and opened again to the public.

It was in August of 1974. I was on the midnights, 11 P.M. to 7 A.M. There were no ships in port, though one was expected in the morning, and no Chicago & North Western freight engine to spot box cars in the center roadway and wake up our neighbors at Lake Point Tower at 3 A.M. Everything was locked up tight, and about 2 A.M., I told my partner that I felt like stretching my legs and would walk out to the end of the pier and back. I put one of our portable radios in my hip pocket and started the 3,600-foot hike to the end.

It was a hot, muggy night, not a hint of the famous lake breeze.

The water in the harbor was like glass, and I could hear the crew operating the Chicago River controlling locks talking and laughing about something. It was clear, calm, hot, humid Chicago weather —the kind of weather that makes Chicagoans go to northern Wisconsin in August—and even 2 A.M. gave no relief.

I was totally alone on the end of the pier, the fire boat that had docked there [was] now tied up at the water filtration plant. I stood for a while watching some pleasure boats and, out against the horizon, a lake ore boat making its way back north as the beacon on the Coast Guard lighthouse at the harbor entrance swept through the night.

On my way back to the office, I decided to walk through the old dance hall. I stopped on entering to allow my eyes to get used to the dark. There was a bright moon that night. I remember noticing how quiet it was in there. The high, cork-lined ceiling absorbed all sound. As I walked across the littered floor, kicking a piece of ceiling material out of my way, I was suddenly aware of the feeling that I was being watched, and watched by someone immediately behind me.

Now, I knew that was impossible; no one could walk across the floor without making noise, yet the feeling was so strong that I whirled around, my hand reaching for the Smith & Wesson at my hip. What was behind me, however, was long past caring about revolver bullets! It was invisible and freezing cold. I felt it pass through me, and I knew what it was. A man.

I turned around, facing my original direction, and stood and tried to sense something—anything—with no result. I took a step forward and was back in the freezing cold again. Another step and I was back in the August heat. You have my attention, pal, I thought, What do you want? I stood still but sensed nothing— no messages of any sort. Well, I thought, I'm not going to let you scare me. And I walked slowly out of the building and back to our office a half-mile west.

When my partner saw me, he asked if I had seen anything interesting, and I answered, *No.* He wouldn't have believed me anyhow.

A year later, I took a lady I knew, a lady with a very high IQ and demonstrated ESP, to the same place. She told me that the man I'd encountered was there waiting for his wife to die. The ballroom had been their dating spot, their nights there his favorite memory.

Phil Wizenick recounted his run-in at Navy Pier's Grand Ballroom in a written account in the spring of 2000.

WAL-MART HAUNTS

Photo by D. Cowan.

The sparkling interior of this ultra-modern marketplace
includes some surprisingly unshakable shadows.

An Off-Price
Poltergeist

THE CHARACTERISTICALLY HUGE WAL-MART store on Route 59 in west suburban Naperville has even more to offer than its numerous counterparts. When the other Wal-Mart locations close their doors for the day, DuPage County delights in the promise of more shopping. For the diapers and drip coffeemakers stocked to the ceilings here are fair game around the clock.

This Wal-Mart never closes.

Before there was Wal-Mart, this was farmland. Like so much of DuPage County—actually, any northern Illinois county—the wind whistled over an expansive prairie here for most of the twentieth century, oceans of crops shimmering in the sunlight, a fierce blackness blanketing the nights.

Then there was Fox Valley Mall.

They built it, and they came, by the thousands, in Broncos and BMWs, stampeding the specialty boutiques and superstores like a starved nation clamoring for sustenance in the form of CDs and Cinnabons. Predictably, Fox Valley wasn't enough to satisfy, and in the years that followed its grand opening, strip malls and their parking lots filled in the surrounding spaces of green and gold for miles, like jigsaw pieces in a giant cinder and asphalt puzzle, leaving little of the prairie that had for centuries sprawled clear to Iowa.

To the suburban mind, the idea of a haunted DuPage mall is a curious one. After all, one may reason, before the mall there was nothing there: no houses, with all their secrets, no insane asylum, no cemetery, no people. But the land may have a better memory than us; for all our good will, we only remember what lasts. The land, though, remembers the transient, the fleeting, the wanderers in the ancient dark.

In the fluorescent anti-culture of today's super-suburbia, remembering the darkness of the land is difficult in itself. With no longtime populations to create and maintain a folklore, recalling the land's ancient secrets may well be impossible. But something lives on here.

At Wal-Mart, employees of the megastore have come to believe that this consumer shrine is the sacred haven of an honest-to-goodness ghost. Since the store's opening, whispers of a resident phantom have been heard among the associates, whose tales from the night shift continue to compel.

The most common occurrences have been of the variety popularly described as "poltergeist activity"; namely, objects which should have been secure fall off shelves for no apparent reason. Less frequent, but more frightening, were the experiences of employees who worked the night shift at the store before it went to 24-hour business days. In those days, the quiet hours were spent working in inventory, stocking, and cleaning. A sparse staff worked silently on the tasks at hand, uninterrupted by the shoppers that now filter through the aisles at all hours, taking advantage of round-the-clock shopping. Baffling then was the sighting by workers of a white-clad woman browsing in the Infants Department in the wee hours. Odder still was the nonchalant air of a girl in a red dress, trying on shoes at 2 A.M. Strangely enough, when one of these "customers" was first seen, the employee would somehow fail to realize the inappropriateness of the person's presence, walking by them unnoticed. A few step later, however, the reality of the time would register, and the worker would try to track down the errant customer with the intention of escorting her out. Such attempts always ended in frustration.

No one—employees, customers, or historians—can offer a clue as to the origins of these mysterious shoppers. A rare speculator seems to recall something about a tragedy that occurred on the site before the store's opening. Whatever the reason, history or imagination has dubbed the white-dressed ghost "Sarah." The sighting of the lady in red, seemingly a one-time occurrence, is generally dismissed by employees as an anomaly.

Wal-Mart's most jarring story comes from a former warehouse worker, who maintains that his crew avoided the warehouse at night complaining of strong unease and of cold spots. Believing the ghost to be that of a man, not a woman, workers there attributed his presence to some accident in the warehouse that long predated the presence of any of the people working third shift.

As another former employee observes, the guesses about the haunting of Wal-Mart are moving "swiftly away from any credible reports and are clearly sailing at full speed into urban legend territory." Still, he finds it interesting that warehouse workers might report of unease, even of cold spots, in the warehouse, specifically in the bins. The warehouse bins lie directly on the other side of the store's rear wall, adjacent to the Boyswear, Girlswear, Infants, and Shoe Departments. Picturing that wall as an arbitrary dividing line, and not an actual barrier, it's largely the same physical territory involved in all of the alleged events. With so much room in this cavernous superstore, why would fabricators limit their imaginations to such a fraction of space?

Former and current Wal-Mart employees volunteered tales of their haunted superstore in exchange for anonymity.

River Grove Haunts

Photo by Elizabeth Wolyniec.

Elizabeth Wolyniec snapped this Polaroid of Our Lady,
Queen of Purity, in a west suburban cemetery.

A Would-Be Witch
Turns Visionary after
a Miraculous Conversion

MANY PEOPLE—RELIGIOUS, NON-RELIGIOUS, and irreligious—have been humbled, baffled, or embittered by the remarkable events reported at places such as Lourdes, France; Fatima, Portugal; and Medjugorje, in the former Yugoslavia. These and other simple towns the world over have been catapulted into enduring international fame by reports of a recurring supernatural phenomenon: the apparition of the Blessed Virgin Mary to apparently unassuming individuals.

In metropolitan Chicago, a Hillside man named Joseph Reinholtz created a local and lasting sensation when, in the early 1980s, he made a pilgrimage to the site of the Medjugorje visions and returned home a visionary himself, inadvertently inspiring the creation of a makeshift shrine at the site of his hometown apparitions in Hillside's Queen of Heaven Cemetery.

Though Reinholtz drew believers to Chicago from all over the country, not all with such gifts are showered with publicity and pilgrims. In fact, a surprising number of unsung individuals claim to have experienced apparitions of religious figures, some with extraordinary regularity.

Elizabeth Wolyniec, a River Grove resident and a virtual native of Chicago's North Shore, has been receiving daily messages from the Blessed Virgin Mary for nearly forty years, a phenomenon which began during her girlhood in Britain, when a dangerous involvement led to a miraculous warning, and a lasting conversion:

Surrey, England is known for the practice of witchcraft and Satanic activities, and for three months I was part of a coven, and that is why Our Lady appeared to me and told me to leave it. I was only able to save nine of my friends, because the others were brutally murdered by the coven head, who was an 18-year-old girl and herself a baptized Christian and the daughter of a Presbyterian minister. I wish not to go into the gory details, because to this very day I still get nightmares from it, even though I have strong love for God, Jesus, and the Holy Spirit and a great devotion to the Blessed Mother Mary under the title of Queen of Purity. I try to discourage young people from practicing Satanism and witchcraft, but many just laugh at me and think I am trying to tell them lies. Many young people, however, have listened to me and have turned back to God, and this makes me feel that I have done some good. I pray for those who laugh, because I know that they can be saved.

It was a very cold, crisp day that November 22, 1961, when I was riding a friend of mine's gelding through a patch of woods outside the county of Surrey. The time was about 4:30 P.M. The gelding tried to bolt, but something or someone made him calm, and he just stood very quietly and did not move.

The air, too, was made calm, and there was unusual stillness. I had ridden in these woods before and never experienced anything like this before in my life. I heard what seemed to be a voice calling me to dismount and come forward to the Scottish pine tree in the middle of the woods, and I obeyed, being very curious. A blue and silver mist shrouded the top of the pine tree, and there stood in the mist an outline of a beautiful lady, and her words were very gentle but urgent, so I knelt and listened while she spoke her words of warning to me. Then she told me that, on the third visit, she would reveal herself to me and that I was to return to the woods on the 22nd of December, 1961, at 4:30 P.M. and she would give me more messages.

I did as she requested, and a friend and her blind brother came with me. My friend's brother drew the outline of the lady in detail, as I've described her. The lady then gave me more urgent messages and twenty-five secrets. When all these are revealed, then much truth will be revealed to the world, and many lives will be saved, and many will be lost.

Our Lady comes to me dressed in a pure white gown, and on her head she wears a Ukrainian Queen's coronet and a gold mantle. Around her waist she has a gold sash that is tied on the left side, and around her left arm she wears a gold and diamond fifteen-decade rosary with a diamond and ruby crucifix at the end of it. On her feet she wears gold and silver slippers, and she has a sweet smile, but sometimes she is sad when she appears.

Our Lord Jesus comes as King of the Universe, and He wears a royal red cape, white tunic, and a king's crown, and on His feet He wears gold sandals. He holds a gold and jeweled scepter in His left hand and an orb in His right hand. Our Lord Jesus is also clothed in a blue and silver cloud; He appears sad sometimes as well. He also gives me messages, and He has also given me twenty secrets to be revealed later, and these, too, will save many lives and many lives will be lost. I always ask for a physical sign when they come to me.

Our Lady's title when she appears to me is Queen of Purity, and her Son Our Lord Jesus' is King of the Universe, and they both appear to me every morning at 4:30 A.M. Here are their messages from this morning, March 22, 2000. Our Lord Jesus spoke first, and then Our Lady spoke next:

My dear Sons and Daughters,

You must learn to love one another and you must work together and help one another, and then you will not have time to fight or steal or hurt one another. You must also obey our Commandments, or your suffering will continue to grow worse and worse. This I say to you as your loving Lord Jesus, because I love you all very much, and it hurts Me to see you all hurt one another.

My dear Children,

You must be more pure in your thoughts, in your hearts, in your bodies, and in your Souls. You must learn to dress more modest and you must be more moral in your thinking, and you must respect each other and do not sell your bodies for profits, because they are temples of God and they cannot be desecrated by any impurities of any kind. Please, my dear, dear Children, be obedient and do as I ask. Thank you for listening to my message.

Elizabeth Wolyniec shared her experiences with the author in a series of letters written between 1999 and 2000.

PRAIRIE AVENUE HAUNTS

Photo by D. Cowan.

This crumbling South Side palace is, some say, as haunted as it looks.

Death Settles Down on Chicago's Easy Street

THE MOVEMENT TO SUBURBANIZE Chicago has not yet overtaken the northeast corner of 18th Street and Prairie Avenue—not quite. Loft residences are metamorphosing here, as everywhere, from the old factories and warehouses, and urban warriors are setting up housekeeping in steel-and-cinder abodes all over the South Loop and beyond, far beyond, past the old Levee district and into Chinatown. Yet, in the dark streets just east of gentrification, the wind can still be heard through the black nights, whistling off Lake Michigan as it did nearly 200 years ago, when the soldiers of Fort Dearborn, and the rough-and-tumble settlers that made their early homes at the mouth of the Chicago River, were butchered by the Potawatomi on the windswept dunes that once sprawled here.

Once upon a time, railway mogul George M. Pullman built a house here, a 35-room wowzer of a house, and, nearly a century after the massacre, commemorated the tragedy with a bronze sculpture placed on its grounds. Disputes still flare over whether this site is truly the same as the massacre's; yet, during construction of the house, workers and passers-by were startled by visions of "settlers" who appeared to float across the broken ground and then vanish into the Prairie Avenue night. Whether or not Pullman's desire to build a monument to the massacre victims stemmed from a wish to stop these apparitions is not clear. What is certain is that they did stop, at least until 1931, nearly ten years after the demolition of the Pullman mansion, when the vandalized statue was relocated to its current home in the Chicago Historical Society. Thereafter, the visions reappeared, decreasing drastically with the installation of a commemorative plaque on the wall of a factory building on the site of the former Pullman home.

The haunting of the historic Prairie Avenue district is, however, accredited to more than vanquished settlers and soldiers. In fact, some of Pullman's own pals are rumored to remain in the homes they built and cherished during their lives of luxury in Chicago's first frou-frou enclave. For, in the waning years of the nineteenth century, Prairie Avenue was the place to be seen; some, even after death, still believe this.

In the 1880s and 1890s, a score of millionaires, the first gentrifiers of the South Loop, turned their backs on the destruction of the Great Fire and built up the area south of the busy downtown business district, staking claim to pieces of land which would give rise to some of the most breathtaking residences America would ever know. It was a true enclave, bounded as it was by the Illinois Central Railroad tracks and Lake Michigan to the east and the evil Levee vice district, an inferno of barrooms and brothels, immediately west. Among those who called Prairie Avenue home was retailing giant Marshall Field, whose lavish life at number 1905 was made only lovelier when his son, Marshall, Jr., married Albertine Huck and moved in down the block to number 1919.

All appeared well until the night of November 22, 1905, when Marshall Field, Jr., alone in the house but for servants, shot himself in the side while seated in his private parlor. As he lay dying in the old Mercy Hospital, Field explained that he had been cleaning his gun while preparing for a Wisconsin hunting trip, and that the revolver had suddenly gone off. But other sources had different information: according to the underground, Field had spent a somewhat typical night before at the notorious Everleigh Club, the queen of all Levee bordellos. Whether a shamefaced suicide or an awkwardly explained accident, Field died several days later, to the grief of his parents (on holiday in New York at the time of the shooting) and the trauma of Albertine and their children. Marshall, Jr. was laid out in the formal parlor at 1919 S. Prairie Avenue and buried at silent but swank Graceland Cemetery, where nearly every one of his neighbors would eventually join him.

In ruins among the remains of the historic district, the William H. Murray house, as Field's mansion was called, still stands today. Rehabbers have given up on it, chased away by the financial disaster of a number of previous attempts at renovation. Outcast from the "chosen" homes of Prairie Avenue (those primped for view by tourists), Marshall, Jr. has all the privacy he could want, and some say he relishes it. In addition to foiling restoration projects, the younger Field is sometimes credited with driving out a rehabilitation center which once set up a boarding house here, a restaurateur with too-high hopes, and even the Prairie Avenue Foundation, whose efforts to acquire the property never quite panned out.

While treasured for its legacy as the home of Chicago's business and philanthropic giants, the Fields, the Pullmans, the Swifts, the Palmers, and other mogul families, Prairie Avenue is equally valued for its architecture. Some of the star pupils of the so-called Chicago School contributed their talents to this stunning district, including Henry Hobson Richardson, who so loved his last commission, the Prairie Avenue house he designed for International Harvester executive John Glessner, that he hung on through dire illness long enough to see the mansion's last stone set. After the building's completion, Richardson promptly died.

Some say the architect was preparing a place for himself. Caretakers and tourists have occasionally reported glimpses of an elusive visitor wandering the rooms of Glessner House, apparently engrossed by the ceilings, lovingly surveying the door frames.

For excellent overviews of the Levee and the Everleigh Club, see "Shutting Down the Levee" in June Skinner Sawyers' Chicago Sketches *and Richard Lindberg's* Return to the Scene of the Crime. *In the latter volume, Lindberg gives some good insights into the case of Marshall Field, Jr.*

CANTIGNY HAUNTS

Author's photo.

The serenity of McCormick's Cantigny Park is
treasured by visitors—and at least one resident.

While the Colonel
Slumbers, a Kindred
Spirit Looks Alive

FIERCELY OPINIONATED, YET AS hotly defensive of others'
freedom of speech, Robert R. McCormick ran a tight editorial ship in his
Chicago Tribune, the newspaper he lorded for almost forty years.
Grandson of the beloved Joseph Medill, the *Tribune*'s publisher,
McCormick freely acknowledged his "inheritance" of the enviable job,
admitting that he knew nothing about the newspaper business.

No matter. McCormick knew what he knew, and through nearly
constant meetings with his editors, he daily stamped the paper with his
distinctive and driven voice.

Military service in the First World War earned McCormick a new
esteem and a new nickname; he was known ever after as "The Colonel,"
a rank dutifully earned in battle and curiously befitting McCormick's
civilian duties as well.

While the Colonel thrived in Chicago, pleased amidst the chaos of
the newsroom, he found increasing comfort in the lavish digs of his
Wheaton farm, Red Oaks, which he inherited from Medill. The simple if
spacious colonial farmhouse was quaint but, in McCormick's eyes,
definitely lacking in creature comforts. Renaming the farm Cantigny,
after the first American victory of McCormick's war (the work of his
own First Division), the Colonel transformed the place into a 35-room
estate house complete with a movie theater: a fitting self-tribute to a man
who championed the promise of the media in any form.

The money for the renovations was easy in coming. Returning to his
editorial post after World War I, McCormick pushed his grandfather's

paper into first place among Midwest circulations. Yet, while McCormick thoroughly enjoyed Cantigny during life, he left the farm to the people of Illinois, bequeathing it as the site of the War Memorial of the First Division, a renowned museum flanked by meticulous gardens.

A serene setting, Cantigny draws many tens of thousands of tourists each year for tours of the Colonel's mansion and walks through the abundantly landscaped grounds. A highlight of these meanders is the Exedra, the tomb of McCormick himself, a placid marble curve as peaceful as the Colonel was outspoken. This polished and pristine monument seems an unfitting place for ghosts. And so it is. Robert McCormick has rested in apparent peace at Cantigny since his death in 1955.

It is, rather, his daughter who roams.

Tucked into a modest grave at the edge of the Colonel's mansion is one of McCormick's cherished favorites, a girl credited with the turning on of lights in her favorite window and visitors' mysterious reports of conversations with a wistful young woman who speaks of her love for the farm and her father, then turns a corner and vanishes.

The author first learned of the Cantigny Park haunts from Dylan Clearfield's Chicagoland Ghosts *(Thunder Bay Press, 1997). Historical background was provided by Cantigny Park and Frank C. Waldrop's* McCormick of Chicago *(Prentice-Hall, 1966).*

HYDE PARK HAUNTS

Photo by Matt Hucke.

Haunting and intricate artwork abounds in Hyde Park's
Oak Woods Cemetery, one of the city's oldest.

A Spirited South Shore Memory

CHICAGO'S SOUTH LAKEFRONT AREA features perhaps Chicago's most fabulous, and far-out, neighborhood. Light years ahead of even the Gold Coast in terms of cosmopolitanism, true sophistication, and style, Hyde Park has lasted seemingly forever as an entrenched but stunningly diverse community. Here are the mega-educated white Protestants who swarm around the University of Chicago; here, too, are blacks of every class, in housing projects and hi-rise penthouses; joining them are paragons of eccentricity: writers, artists, actors, and musicians of every kind; thrown in for good measure are politicians, players, and regular folks by the thousands, engrossed in the business of life, be it researching the divine at Catholic Theological Union or downing a zombie and a plate of chicken wings at the House of Tiki.

Annexed by the city of Chicago in the late nineteenth century, Hyde Park began as a beautiful town within a city, surrounded by the sprawling Victorian expanses of Jackson and Washington Parks. Soon after the township's adoption, the University of Chicago grew from land donated by super-philanthropical Marshall Field and John D. Rockefeller's money. Hyde Park would forever bear the tell-tale mark of these ultra-privileged, in its institutions, in its landscape, and in its homes.

Lee Grossman* was one of thousands of children raised in one of these very cushy, but slightly off-kilter, Hyde Park houses. Though his family was relatively well-to-do, thanks to the business savvy of his entrepreneurial father, not even they could properly keep up their ridiculously lavish digs on Kenwood Avenue— a mansion outfitted with every luxury imaginable, which showed signs of its long past in the crumbling plaster, the accursed plumbing, and the non-paying tenants.

Grossman explains:

I, too, lived in a haunted house. It was on the South Side of Chicago, in the 5200 block of south Kenwood. It was a twelve-room house: three stories and a full basement. We had—I don't know—[what] might have been half a dozen fireplaces in the house, and what happened to me there happened back in the 1940s, in the Second World War, when I was quite a young child.

The University of Chicago might have title to the house at this time. At that particular time, we didn't own the house. My dad had rented it with an option to buy, and he was not a handyman, and he was spending tons of money, putting it into this older house for upkeep. We had to do all kinds of painting, and the plumbers were continuously there. It was a beautiful place to grow up in, but it was definitely haunted.

Now, my father—we—tried to trace who owned this house, and it was built in the late 1880s or early 1890s, and my dad said it had been used as a gambling den. Now, the reason he found this out was that he had been head of all the bookmaking on the South and Southwest Sides of Chicago (which was semi-legal in those days and quite profitable), and he talked to somebody who talked to somebody who told him it was one of the first places used for gambling in Hyde Park. You won't find that in the record books anywhere.

Also, when they were plastering, they found some bumps in the wall which my dad thought they would dig out (thinking they were screws or something) and plaster over. But my dad identified them as two .32 caliber rounds from a revolver.

After I had left the house, they had more contractors in, and they found a space in the house—broke into a hidden room. It might have been behind the fireplace. It was dusty, had never been used, and there was a postcard that just said, you know, "Wish you were here," posted from San Francisco, 1912.

My mother and grandmother always claimed that the house was catacombed with sliding doors, secret passageways, and trap doors. I don't know if they ever found any more; they didn't look any further than that. But my dad was suspicious that there were other places in the basement and through the upstairs because of measuring the dimensions of the rooms.

At the time I was growing up there, we had a servant—Old Julius—who lived in the house. There were servant quarters in back, and he would do things like stoke the furnace. And there was a part-time maid, and there was Howie—a family relative who was in the Air Force. He had the Air Force version of shell shock. He was home on leave, and he never did go back to combat, fortunately.

So I was lying in my room one day around six o'clock or so; before that I had taken a nap. And for some reason I woke up and turned over—something prompted me to roll over and look at the door, and the door swung open to my room, and a man entered my room, and he was only in my vision—I've replayed this in my mind a million times, frame by frame like a camera—a very, very few seconds. He crossed the floor at a diagonal, walked over to the closet, opened the closet door and walked in and shut the door.

The man that I observed looked at me as he crossed the floor, and he wasn't walking exactly; his feet were almost like on roller skates; he made a strange motion as he went across the floor.

He was a soldier. He had a khaki shirt and khaki trousers; I don't think he was wearing a tie. He had reddish-brown hair, and it was combed in a pomp in the front like they combed 'em in the 1940s. It was kind of longish but then no sideburns and kind of short in the back. I remember every detail like it was yesterday.

His face was icy and bluish. You couldn't see through him, but it was all white and blue like it was frozen, and when he looked directly at me, there were no eyes. They were like two black coals, one in each eye.

I got up, ran to the closet, opened the door, looked in, and there was nothing there. My dad must have had a hundred suits hanging in there (he used it to store his suits). I shut the door, ran downstairs, and my grandmother was there and I told her. Of course, a little child saying, *There was a man in my room—* nobody pays any attention.

Now I'm going to go fast forward a moment here and say that, years later, I talked to relatives who had seen this very same soldier—same khaki clothes, same everything I described—independently of me and never mentioned it because they didn't want to scare a little child.

My mother came home late one day with my father who owned a large—well, they called 'em night clubs in those days—at 51st and Lake Park Boulevard. He would walk home early in the morning after he'd close up. (In those days, totally safe. In those days, there was nobody in the neighborhood but very young and very old people—male and female.) When [my father] came in, [my mother] walked in to [tend] the fireplace which was going for him to keep warm, and a man got up out of a chair in what they called the sitting room. This man walked to the back and disappeared, and that was the same identical soldier my mother saw.

The other incident that happened to me—melodramatic—is that this thing tried to kill me, or at least do me bodily harm. I was standing at the staircase somewhat after this, and I felt a hand on my back. I turned and looked, and I was pushed down the staircase but not hurt. There was not even a bruise.

I got up, told somebody in the house—at the time, my mother or my grandmother—and they said, you know, *Oh, you fell down, be more careful.* And I said, *No, I was pushed. . . . I could feel the hand on my back.*

Old Julius, who was the family caretaker, was a superstitious, older black man, much beloved by the family, and he was in his late 60s. He was down one morning stoking the furnace, and this thing (we couldn't get heads or tails out of him what, but we think it was soldier) came out of the coal bin and walked towards him.

At the time, we were having breakfast because it was early in the morning. Julius's job was to take the clinkers out of the furnace, put in coal, and get it going good. Up the staircase he came from the basement, ran by, jumped over the fence—and we did not see him for about two weeks. My dad spotted him standing on the street corner by the house drinking out of a bottle of gin two weeks later. He went over and said, *Julius, why don't you come home, you've been gone so long*—and got the story. And Julius was totally petrified.

We couldn't keep the maid either because she saw something, and she wouldn't tell us what it was.

The other thing that happened was that I was in the basement with my father and Julius and—I don't know why—I looked up and it looked like there was a saw sawing a piece out of the ceiling. It went right around circular, and the chunk fell out like it was only plaster, it wasn't wood. I stepped to the side and it missed me. If it would have hit me, it would not have hurt me. But I obviously was the target.

Also, I can remember sitting upstairs with my grandmother and we heard [something] like a brigade upstairs stomping across the floor. We sat there a half hour and listened to it. Finally, my grandmother—brave person that she was—went upstairs and looked around, and there was nothing.

An alternate name has been used at the request of the witness, who shared his account with the author in a tape-recorded narrative given to the author in the spring of 2000.

O'HARE FIELD HAUNTS

Photo courtesy of Bertog's Fire Photos.

Victims of this unspeakable accident at O'Hare Field reportedly
sought shelter and aid at nearby homes—though all died instantly.

Bringing in the Dead

ON A GLORIOUS DAY in late May, 1979, several hundred passengers at Chicago's O'Hare International Airport waited aboard American Airlines Flight 191, a McDonnell Douglas DC-10, for departure to Los Angeles. It was the Friday before Memorial Day and, despite being cramped on board a commercial flight on such a fine afternoon, the travelers were glad to have escaped the bustle of the world's busiest airport on one of its busier days. The passengers and crew of Flight 191 were in the most capable of hands: those of Walter Lux, an expert DC-10 pilot with some 22,000 hours of flight time. The plane itself was no rookie either, having traveled 20,000 smooth, solid hours since its first trip. Everyone on board settled in for an easy ride, surely dreaming about the long weekend ahead.

At a minute before 3 P.M., the plane was cleared to begin its taxi to the runway's holding point. Then, at 3:02 P.M., with everything go, the DC-10 started down the runway. All was smooth and usual until, just after takeoff, one of the engines lost power.

The events that followed are legendary in the annals of aviation history. A strange, vaporous substance began pouring from the fuel lines where the engine finally tore away from the wing, taking the pylon with it. Despite the loss, the wing soon stabilized and 191 continued its sure ascent. Briefly. Not ten seconds later, at a height of about 300 feet, the craft began to bank left, first slightly, then sharply. The nose of the plane fell, losing control. Flight 191 dove earthward.

The port wingtip hit ground in sync with a massive explosion that totally destroyed the plane. All 271 passengers and crew members were killed instantly, along with two residents of a nearby trailer park, resulting in the deadliest air disaster in American history.

Bewildered by the enormity of the tragedy, Chicagoans watched in disbelief as the news reports detailed the events of the afternoon. The nation joined Chicago in demanding answers from the airline, the airfield, and the National Transportation Safety Board: Why, when ordinarily a plane could finish its flight with one missing engine, did the loss of Flight 191's engine seal its doom? The question would initiate a grueling investigation into the flawed maintenance methods leading to the crash of that supposedly serviceable DC-10. But the answers were long in coming and, meanwhile, residents of the area surrounding O'Hare had puzzles of their own to solve.

In the hours after the crash, a number of houses in the far northwest corners of the city echoed with the sounds of knocking at their doors and windows. Residents who responded, among them a number of retirees and off-duty police and firefighters, found no sign of visitors. The mysterious rappings occurred again and again. Neighbors returning home that evening experienced the same knockings. Over the next several weeks, sporadic reports of unseen callers continued to be turned in to the police. At last, as the crash site was finally cleared and the final strips of detective's tape removed from its boundaries, peace came again to the Northwest Siders, who could only pray that their transient neighbors had found a better place to stay. They had. For the most part.

Since the crash of Flight 191 in the spring of '79, a few lone souls have apparently lingered in the vicinity of their final hour, sending up wails and moans from the field where they met their end. Others are said to wander, sometimes straying as far as the cemeteries of Rest Haven and St. Johannes, both on the grounds of the airfield itself. There, among the weathered stones of these noisy expanses, mourners are comforted by unseen hands on their arms and shoulders, and sighs are heard in the wake of the whoosh of departing flights overhead.

Inside the airport, at least one of 191's passengers remains, forever retracing his final actions before boarding the doomed DC-10. For the past 20 years, at a pay phone near the terminal's lounge, passengers at O'Hare have watched as a somber male figure wraps up a last-minute conversation, turns expectantly toward the ill-fated gate, takes a few determined steps . . . and vanishes.

The story of the aftermath of the crash of Flight 191 was related to the author in a number of anonymous personal accounts. Background on the crash was provided by www.AirDisaster.com, *a useful resource for those interested in both military and commercial flight accident history. The author was alerted to the haunting of St. Johannes as a result of the Crash of '79 by Ed Geary, whose report was supported by accounts.*

"Light" House Haunts

Somber News from
a Suburban Oracle

GHOST LIGHTS, OR SPOOK lights, as they are called in some parts of the United States, are a curious classification of phenomena. Occurring in many parts of the world, often with amazing regularity, these luminous balls may be seen along many suburban and rural roads. Local folks have long gathered at the 95th Street Overlook in southwest suburban Chicago to gaze at a mysterious light hovering in the woods across Maple Lake and have run from those sighted at notorious Bachelors Grove Cemetery, sometimes in broad daylight. Serious Chicago light watchers have traveled many miles to witness the world-famous but elusive lights that have glimmered for years in Joplin, Missouri, and Marfa, Texas.

Though ghost lights in the classic sense are quite visible to the eye, sometimes drawing crowds of regulars to watch them on Saturday nights, enigmatic lights are not limited to this variety. In fact, far more common is the appearance of strange lights on still photos and, less commonly, videotape *after* development of the film. That is, at the time of the photograph or taping, no light is visible to the eye; yet, photos or film reveal so-called orbs of semi-opaque light or darting shots of translucence. Many neophyte ghost researchers are spending a lot of money and time on the exploration of these unexplainable energy sources, on the theory that they may represent formless spirits betraying themselves through their own radiant energy.

Far less common than either of these phenomena, however, is the puzzling luminescence that occurs in real time, not on film or photos, in a personal setting and spontaneously. For while hundreds are constantly thrilling to the predictable appearance of ghost lights at outdoor sites around the world, others are troubled by the sudden, fleeting, and private appearance of such lights: lights that seem to have a mind of their own, are as far from explanation as anything in human experience, and as close as one's own bedroom.

Mary Gorman, a Canadian by birth, has lived in southwest suburban Midlothian for 40 years. But less than a day after her 1959 move to her longtime home, she became aware of a strangeness about the place. Only about 20 years old, the house had little to offer in the way of grisly or mysterious history, but the neglect of former owners had taken a toll, and the Gormans spent their first day in the house trucking out a generation of trash, working long and hard into the evening, preparing the house for proper habitation.

Then came the first lights-out, and the first of many less-than-normal nights:

> I was awakened in the middle of the night by the sound of a baby crying. I was at that time eight months pregnant. The crying continued every night until my baby was born. At that time, it abruptly stopped.

> Everything was quiet for about a year. Then, one night, I had been sound asleep when something woke me, and I was startled to see a perfect circle of light traveling all around the door frame. It moved from the bottom of the frame, going up to the top, then turned and followed the top of the frame across to the edge, then turned again and began to go down on the other side. I tried to find an origin for the light, but failed.

> The following morning I received a call to let me know that my uncle had died in the night.

> Again, all was quiet for a while. Then it happened once more, only this time there were three perfect circles. These circles did the same thing as the single circle had done in my earlier experience, but with one following the other in perfect order.

> The call that came the following morning informed us that my husband's cousin, who had lived with us in the house for a short time, had been murdered in an alley in Chicago.

> The third time I saw this light there was, once again, only one circle.

> This time, the morning brought news of my brother-in-law. Though only in his early 40s, he had suffered a sudden and fatal

heart attack.

The account of the "light" house prognostications was related to the author by Mary Gorman in a written account in the summer of 2000.

BEVERLY SHORES HAUNTS

Author's photo.

An eagle eye can pick out the Chicago skyline on the horizon, viewed across Lake Michigan from this sand dune at Porter Beach in Indiana.

Alice in Duneland

WHEN SUMMER COMES TO Chicago, Lake Michigan warming under the midwestern sun in the early days of June, city dwellers pour onto the town's beaches by the thousands for a breath of air and a splash of fresh water. Despite the ethereal feel of the lakefront in summer, the blue stretching to the horizon, the billows of cloud and sand, this is, alas, still Chicago. As such, the city has little to offer the urbanite longing for windswept days on Cape Cod or Martha's Vineyard. To make the experience of Lake Michigan a bit more oceanic, Chicagoans have long fled the city—today by car, in former years by the South Shore Line on the Illinois Central Railroad tracks—to the sand dunes of the Indiana and Michigan coastlines. Here, despite the smoke-stacks of the nearby steel mills, the towering mountains of sand painted with prairie grass offer an authentic getaway, just over the famed Skyway bridge joining Illinois and Indiana. Here, the magic of the old summertime lives on, little more than a stone's throw away from the bustle.

Sometime around 1915, fishermen off the Indiana shoreline began making detours from their established routes in hopes of catching a glimpse of a mysterious young woman. "Diana of the Dunes," a legendarily beautiful girl who had run away from home to live in a run-down beachfront shanty, was rumored to swim nude off the beach where she made her solitary home. The sight of her lithe, bronzed form running on the sand to dry was apparently well worth the detour. When city reporters got wind of the tale, they tracked down the girl, finding not a tanned and toned young beauty queen, but a quiet and frail woman of 34.

Alice Mabel Gray, a Massachusetts' prep school graduate, had been Phi Beta Kappa at the University of Chicago; after graduation, she had taken a job editing an astronomy magazine. While stories had grown about a tragic love affair which sent Gray fleeing to the Dunes in despair, the truth was that she had lost part of her eyesight and could no longer attend to her meticulous work.

An avid naturalist, she had spent much of her college years surveying the Dunes area, cataloging its native flora and fauna. With little opportunity in a scarce job market, Gray opted for a life of freedom in the place she loved best. Setting up housekeeping in an old fisherman's home, Gray eventually invited in a mysterious stranger, the estranged son of an upper-class Indiana family, to make his home with her on the beach. Handy and devoted (despite a string of criminal acts), the man fixed up Gray's crumbling house and helped put food on the table. According to the more romantic legends, he built boats and furniture, which he sold to support Alice.

Though the truth about Alice, and her mysterious houseguest, is still sketchy at best, no one doubts that the man taken in by her was a hot-tempered scoundrel. When a half-burnt corpse was found on the beach nearby, all fingers pointed to Alice's man. When a deputy came to the house to question the couple, he was shot by the suspect. Alice was also injured in the skirmish, ending up in a Gary hospital.

Though Alice's friend was not charged, the couple's magic Duneland life was over. Curiosity-seekers descended on their beach home, eager for a look at the suntanned pin-up and her ill-tempered protector. Forced to move, the two ultimately relocated to Texas after real-estate developers drove them out of their second home. Returning to the Dunes several years later, the pair lived out a miserable life with an enigmatic daughter, Bonita. After giving birth to a second girl, Bluebell, Gray endured an abusive life with her longtime lover in a ramshackle house near the beach she'd always adored. She is said to have died in the winter of 1925 in the arms of her children's father.

Talk spread far and wide about Diana of the Dunes and the treachery that surrounded her strangely placid, poignantly tragic figure. Talk spread, too, about the possibility that, after her death, Alice lived on.

For nearly three-quarters of a century, visitors to the Indiana Dunes State Park, where "Diana" made her former home, have reported seeing a slight and bedraggled feminine figure stealing over the sands at twilight, at times plunging into the Lake Michigan waters, even in the freezing months. Others, approaching the famous shack where she lived (now demolished), have marveled at the sound of crying emanating from the abandoned homestead.

Perhaps the most stirring legend, however, is one which echoes that of New England's Grey Man. For just as East Coast vacationers look for the Grey Man to warn them of impending hurricanes, native Indiana residents claim that Alice Gray, too, appears only before severe storms, her gentle and naturalistic spirit guiding her fellow Dunes lovers, warning fisherman and pleasure-boaters to steer for home.

Specific biographical information on Diana of the Dunes (Alice Mabel Gray) was provided by rangers at the Indiana Dunes State Park Visitors Center and by Beth Scott and Michael Norman's volume, Haunted Heartland.

VICTORIAN HOUSE HAUNTS

Author's photo.

This treasure in transition has long echoed with past misdeeds.

Eerie Antiques Flavored
a Favorite Haunt

A NUMBER OF YEARS ago, in the days when Chicago's Lakeview neighborhood was still considered offbeat, the Victorian House Restaurant sat on the northwest corner of Halsted Street and Belmont Avenue. Long popular among the genteel and genteel-minded women of both city and suburbs, this nineteenth-century oasis was a place to make a day of, thanks in large part to its companion antique shop housed in an adjoining painted lady of a house, somewhat out of place among the streamlined boutiques and run-down frame houses and brick flats of west Belmont.

Cherished by patrons for its elegant fare and sumptuous surroundings, the Victorian House was known not only for its beauty, but also for its bogeymen. For it was here that, soon after the house's completion, the original owner was murdered. After new owners moved in, four people were killed in an attic fire. Thereafter, the place was abandoned as a residence and later transformed into an antique-hunter's heaven. Treasure seekers had to be willing to endure a few willies from the start, however, as pale faces were rumored to stare out of mirrors, accompanied by the fall of footsteps across the attic floor.

During the restaurant's heyday, many a customer climbed the stretch of steps of Victorian House Antiques in hopes of spying a glimmer of the ghosts said to walk its halls. Dripping with treasures both rare and run-of-the-mill, the house seemed infinitely hauntable and, indeed, over the years a number of visitors were privy to the antics of one or more lingering spirits. Colleen Vaccaro, a native Chicagoan living in Oswego, was one of many who reveled in the charm of the Victorian House. Yet, during the years of her patronage, Vaccaro was unaware of the ghost stories which lodged in the darkest corners of the restaurant's adjoining shop.

No matter. During some browsing time one fine afternoon, the house's invisible inhabitant decided to make a personal introduction, waiting for a moment when Vaccaro became separated from the rest of her party:

> The Victorian House was a place filled with both beautiful antiques and charm. I especially recall the lovely collection of antique crystal the owner had displayed throughout. In an adjoining dining room, there was a spectacular glass ceiling that had once been in one of Al Capone's speakeasies. An added appeal to this destination in the city was that, housed next door in a lovely Victorian house, was the Victorian House Antiques Shop, a place filled with quality antiques and a knowledgeable owner to boot, who volunteered any information he could on the pieces he sold.

> One Saturday afternoon, my mother, my sister, and myself decided to lunch and "antique hunt" at the Victorian House and its sister store. Being that the shop was housed in this lovely old row-style home, there were a couple of floors and numerous rooms to cover. My mother, sister, and I ventured upstairs, noting the protrusion in the wall at the top of the stairs which, as we had been told by the owner, had allowed for caskets to make the trip down the staircase more easily in the old days—an interesting use for what I'd thought was just an architectural embellishment! In any case, we found ourselves in the second-floor room that overlooked Belmont Avenue. We shared comments about some furniture that was housed in the room and, while my mother and sister moved on to the next room, I lingered, admiring the detail in some of the larger furnishings.

> The afternoon light filtered in and, along with admiring the antiques, I found myself in a dreamy state, wondering who'd lived in the lovely home and what stories it held. I probably would have remained like this longer; however, as quickly as the pleasant feeling of the time I was spending had come upon me, a feeling that I was being watched took over and sent any feeling of pleasantry away.

> I've heard it said that, when there is a ghost in a room, the hair on your neck stands on end. Well, I just had the feeling that someone was standing behind me and wishing me out of that room and

quickly. I know I acted promptly on my instincts and joined my mother and sister in the other room. And I remember thinking there was no doubt in my mind that something or someone had not wanted me in that room, and that I left there feeling unsettled at the experience.

I really wasn't surprised when, a while later, I read a reader's letter to a Chicago newspaper columnist, asking the location of a haunted antique shop in the city. The reply? The Victorian House. And I remember thinking that at least my feeling in the room that day had somehow been validated.

Colleen Vaccaro's experience at the old Victorian House Antiques shop was recounted to the author in a written statement in the summer of 2000.

STARVED ROCK HAUNTS

Author's photo.

While historians labor to preserve this state park's heritage,
Starved Rock tends to its own past—in its own way.

Lingering Echoes of the Illini Ordeal

IN THE EARLY DAYS of autumn, 1873, several thousand Illinoisans made a tedious trip by farm horse buggies and sleekly-led carriages through the canyons and bluffs of Utica along the Illinois River. Their destination: the grassy base of storied Starved Rock, where they were to spread their picnics and listen to historians tell tales of the region, from its Christianization (courtesy of Father Marquette, "The Black Robe") to the name-gaining night when the Illini Indians were driven to the bluff by their allied enemies, who aimed to starve them to death.

The visitors who gathered in Utica that afternoon heard not history but legends, for no written, first-hand account existed to relate, or reason, the horrific events behind "Starvation Rock." Instead, archivists gathered tales told them by men like Shick Shack, an elusive old Indian chief who, in 1831 and at the age of 104, told his own version of the story to a nine-year-old boy named Perry Armstrong, who would grow up to write a respectable account of the Black Hawk War and tell Shick Shack's tale to that eager autumn throng 40 years later.

Armstrong's tale, and the necessary grain of salt, have been passed on to visitors at Starved Rock State Park ever since the first piece of the park, 280 acres, was purchased by the state in December, 1911. Acre by acre, with bottom-of-the-barrel funds, additions were made throughout the early years of the twentieth century. Today, the park spans a three-mile acreage along the south bank of the Illinois River, complete with hiking trails, cabins, a campground, and, for the less adventurous, a cavernous, fireplace-studded lodge and convention center.

Despite the amenities, the name and the story behind it remain.

By the early eighteenth century, on the eve of the chase to the Rock, the Illini had been nearly exterminated as a result of constant warfare with enemy tribes, namely the Fox, who routinely slaughtered and burned Illini and scalped and killed countless French traders, taking their furs as booty. The Illini responded in kind to Fox attacks, trading their own bitter violence for the brutality of their enemies. By the fall of 1722, the conflict had reached such intensity that Fox allies, including the Macaoutins, the Kickapoos, the Winnebagos, the Sauks, and even Sioux and Abenakies, joined the tribe at the foot of a steep bluff which banked the Illinois River and drove the last of the Illini Indians to its summit.

There, the Illini stayed, the mass of enemy tribes swarming on one side, the fatal dive into the swirling Illinois River awaiting on another, sharp drop-offs into rocky crags closing off any other chance of escape. As the Illini dwindled from starvation, thirst, and smallpox, the Fox allies made camp on what is now called Camp Rock or Lover's Leap, a bluff east of Starved Rock. When, out of sheer frustration and panic, a number of the Illini attempted to escape, the woods around the Rock rang with their death cries, as their enemies bludgeoned and speared the fugitives. Others were spared, only to be burned at the stake as a sign of victory.

It is yet unknown how long the Illini were kept prisoner on Starved Rock. Their torment, however, is well noted by those same word-of-mouth accounts that have kept the story alive. William Hickling, the first mayor of nearby Ottawa, had heard of the Illini agony from Meachelle, a Potawatomi chief who was a boy at the time of the tragedy. Likely a Camp Rock lookout for his elders, the youngster was not too young to realize what the Illini were enduring. Hickling, and other historians who have shared his passion for the story of the Rock, have told of Meachelle's own dark memories:

> [He] did not know either, how long the Illini remained in the
> craggy death trap. Far away on the other side of the river were
> the corn fields and food supplies of no use to them, in their agony
> of hunger. The blue waters of the Illinois, filled with game fish
> swirled below the rock, but again [this] was a mockery.

The devastation of the starvation, however, did not bring an end to the Illini. A number of accounts contend that nearly a dozen escaped, stole their enemies' canoes, and sought shelter with friendly tribes and French traders along the river. Such tales speak of a miracle of snow that fell one night, covering the tracks of the fleeing Illini, granting them time enough for escape before the discovery of their feat by the enraged Fox.

Yet, while the Illini endured their trial at "Starvation Rock," more danger lay ahead in the endless territorial warfare and still more hunger, such as they endured during the nightmarish winter in the 1770s

> when the game starved because of the deep snows and the Indians huddled day after day in the miserable huts enduring the combined terrors of a merciless winter and famine.

For nearly 300 years, the expanse known today as Starved Rock State Park has harbored some of the most compelling of all Illinois ghostlore. The ancient tales of the Rock have fostered reports of cries echoing in the forests and canyons surrounding the Rock, presumably the death shrieks of the vainly fleeing Illini. Visitors canoeing on the Illinois River are baffled by the screams materializing out of thin air as they sweep through the shadowy waters beneath the "Starvation Rock." And hikers who stop for the view from Camp Rock to examine the etchings in the stone at Lover's Leap search in vain for the source of hushed voices on the trail behind them.

While the history books still struggle for a credible account of the Illini ordeal at Starved Rock, visitors to the park seem to need little convincing of the reality of their struggle. As they travel through the sprawl of forested canyon in all seasons, they are haunted by the simple, crumbling tales of Shick Shack and Meachelle. And while the park has erected a fine memorial to the memory of the Illini's ordeal, detailing the events of nearly three hundred years ago, the towering reaches of Starved Rock itself seem to need no reminder.

I learned of the haunting of Starved Rock State Park in Dylan Clearfield's Chicagoland Ghosts. *I am indebted to Mr. Clearfield and to C.C. Tisler's little volume,* Starved Rock: Birthplace of Illinois *(n.p., n.p., 1956), which provided the historical background and folk accounts mentioned of Starved Rock. It was Tisler who recounted the anniversary picnic held at the Rock in 1873, which aimed to celebrate the 200th year since the arrival of Marquette and Joliet. Tisler confides a wry event of the picnic day: "The original speaker . . . was to have been Supreme Court Justice Sydney Breese, but the judge begged off from the assignment, saying his eyesight was failing and he could not read manuscript as well as he should. . . . [A] Republican editor commented tartly that Judge Breese then had no business being on the bench, if he could not read manuscript."*

CRIPPEN HOUSE HAUNTS

Author's photo.

Local historians claim that this landmark home
plays host to an anonymous ancestor.

A Neighborhood Treasure Lives Again

WHEN **T**ONY **ENCOUNTERED** an invisible something at Crippen House, the 160-year-old "new" headquarters of the Norwood Park Historical Society, he was already acquainted with the Unknown. For five years, he and his wife, Barbara, had lived in an old farmhouse at Austin and Meade Avenues—a house that included one uninhabitable room. Barbara had lived in the place alone for a while, having purchased it five years earlier. No stranger to weird houses, the couple had lived for years in the Marmora Avenue house where Chicago serial killer John Wayne Gacy had grown up. In that home, Barbara and her family had heard a number of sounds in the basement, including the scrape against the floor of chairs from a chrome kitchen set even after they threw the set out.

Years later, while housecleaning her own Meade Avenue house, Barbara would come upon a certain upstairs room and routinely begin dusting it. Each week, she was annoyed to find that a carved, wooden box she kept there would have its lid inverted. After five years of flipping the lid back over each week, it suddenly dawned on her that someone else had been doing the inverting. Dating Tony at the time, Barbara asked him to take the box home with him, to see if it would behave the same way at his house. It did not. The box was returned to its place in the mysterious room and immediately resumed its bizarre behavior.

Before the revelation about the room, Barbara had unconsciously avoided its use; afterwards, the disuse became a bit more purposeful. When she married Tony soon after, her new husband began experiencing unusual phenomena as well. While taking courses at Columbia College, he would at times wake up in the morning to find the textbooks he'd stacked neatly the night before scattered across the hallway. Studying late in the evening, he'd hear rappings on the window. When the latter phenomenon became annoying, he'd tell the rapper to stop. Usually, whatever it was complied.

Meanwhile, Barbara continued having her own run-ins with their non-paying tenant. Returning home one afternoon after shopping with her brother, she found the living room curtains stretched out over the furniture, a discovery which led her to force her brother to check the house for intruders. None were found. Though Barbara didn't feel any real discomfort living in their home, when she and Tony had a baby, she refused to use the taboo room as a nursery, instead placing the newborn's crib in the couple's own bedroom.

After Tony and Barbara moved out of the house several years ago, settling into another, more "comfortable" place on the city's Northwest Side, a new family moved into their old Meade Avenue farmhouse. Not long after, an old neighbor asked the couple if anyone had died in the home; the new owners had been asking around, presumably after their own close encounters.

Avid historians, both Barbara and Tony have devoted much time and energy to the restoration of the ancient Crippen House, which was reopened to the public in the spring of 2000 after massive structural, electrical, and other renovations, thanks to public grants supplemented with local donations. Before the reopening of the house, the couple spent time working on projects there for the Norwood Park Historical Society. Tony often found himself working alone, as he was one afternoon when he had a lot of photocopying to finish.

Tony had been copying documents and other papers in the basement of the house, working among the old dress forms and other vintage paraphernalia stored in the space. As the pages zipped through the machine, he suddenly heard a voice say, almost accusingly, *Hey!* Turning towards it, he was surprised to see no one there.

Thinking the caretaker, who was working outside, had come in, Tony sought him out. Glancing out a nearby window, however, he saw the man playing with his dog out near the street, a distance of well over 100 feet.

Brushing off the incident, Tony went upstairs to gather some more papers for copying. In an upper room, he heard the voice again: *Hey!* Convinced that someone was playing a joke, he searched for a culprit, again finding no one in or near the house.

When Tony heard the voice a third time back in the basement, again calling *Hey!*, he ignored it, finished up his work, cleaned up calmly, and left.

Ghosthunters hearing Tony's story will be tempted to chalk the experience up to the disturbance in the Crippen House spirits as a result of the extensive renovations.

Not so fast.

Unlike most such stories, where home remodeling projects conjure up suspicious ancestors who aim to observe and approve of the changes, Tony's encounter in the building's basement occurred long before the intensive renovation started.

Today, Crippen House is doing well, its 160 years hardly showing, thanks to widespread efforts on its behalf. The interior cosmetic work has begun, and the old homestead is solidly on the path to complete restoration. Whether the house's audible invisibles will remain here after the Society really settles in, tour groups streaming through its halls with greater and greater frequency, remains an unanswerable question. Only time, of course, will tell. In the meantime, Tony and other Crippen House workers can confirm that an unseen caretaker is still keeping an eye on the place.

Tony and Barbara furnished their tales of the supernatural Northwest Side, including the happenings at Crippen House, in telephone interviews conducted in the summer of 2000.

CAMPBELL AVENUE HAUNTS

Author's photo.

This unassuming Lincoln Square street is said to
replay an historic neighborhood mystery.

A Ragged Stranger
and a Hapless Wanderer

LONGTIME *CHICAGO DAILY NEWS* journalist Ben Hecht is remembered by the world for his enormously successful efforts as a novelist, playwright, and screenwriter. Yet, the *Front Page* co-author won over his hometown with his own provincialism and wonderfully celebratory, sometimes bitter tales of the city. Published in sync with the onset of his national fame in a daily column entitled "One Thousand and One Afternoons," Hecht's year of sketches painted a stunning portrait of the Chicago he observed each day, pounding the pavements as a regular Joe—a regular Joe with a wistfully appreciative, keenly poetic pen.

Though Hecht was discovered by national critics with the release of his novel *Erik Zorn* three months after the first of his "Afternoons" sketches was released, the pieces continued to appear on editor Henry Justin Smith's desk. Despite the clamor for manuscripts, the lure of syndicates, the avalanche of mail from critics, fans, and maniacs, Hecht churned out the "Afternoons" column like a man addicted.

In his introduction to a collection of the sketches (appropriately titled *1001 Afternoons in Chicago*), first published in 1922, Smith recalls Hecht's devotion to the column:

> We wondered how he did it. We saw him in moods when he almost surrendered, when the strain of juggling with novels, plays and with contracts, revises, ad-blurbs, sketches, nearly finished "One Thousand and One Afternoons." But a year went by, and through all that year there had not been an issue of *The Chicago Daily News* without a Ben Hecht sketch. And still the manuscripts dropped down regularly on the editor's desk. Comedies, dialogues, homilies, one-act tragedies, storiettes, sepia panels, word-etchings, satires, tone-poems, fuges, bourrees—something different every

day. . . . Stories seemingly born out of nothing, and written—to judge by the typing—in ten minutes.

While Hecht shrugged his sketches off as "hack-work, done for a meal ticket," his editor knew better, knew that they flowed from "a strictly artistic inspiration and gained further momentum from the need of expression, from pride in the subtle use of words, from an ardent interest in the city and its human types." This interest would remain with Ben Hecht throughout his celebrated career, his skilled eyes seeing deeper than most into people and their actions, into the everyday events that, under his awesome scrutiny, sometimes proved quite extraordinary.

Such was the case with Hecht's view of Carl Wanderer, who returned home with his pregnant, 19-year-old wife of eight months, Ruth, on the evening of June 21, 1920 after a night at the old Pershing (now Davis) Theater. At the door to their house at 4732 N. Campbell Avenue, Wanderer was about to turn on the vestibule light to better see the keyhole. At that point, a voice said, *Don't turn on the light.*

Confronted by a would-be mugger, the Wanderers might have reacted in any of a thousand ways. Unbeknownst to the so-called "ragged stranger," however, Wanderer was packing. He drew his pistol, startling the holdup man into opening fire. Wanderer's wife was killed by the unknown criminal; the mugger was shot by Wanderer in self-defense.

Well, that was Wanderer's story, anyway.

Penning the tale of the tragedy for *The Chicago Daily News*, Ben Hecht wasn't buying it, even as he wrote it. With Hecht hot on its heels, the story became a sensation.

Lincoln Square resident Bob Wilson*, a graduate researcher who lives near the infamous murder site, tells the story of Wanderer's run-in with the so-called "ragged stranger"—and what happened next:

> 'The first shot blew him across the hallway,' Wanderer told
> Ben Hecht. 'Then I couldn't see him, but I knew where he'd
> landed and I let him have three more.' But this simple story of
> a murdering thief getting what was coming to him soon started
> to fall apart. The dead mugger was identified as Edward Masters,
> a well-known gunman; Wanderer acted suspiciously unconcerned
> about the death of his wife; and it was soon revealed that the same

gun was used in both murders—and had been in Wanderer's
possession the day before.

Wanderer, a recent veteran who was cited as the best pistol shot
of his battalion, soon confessed to the crime, saying that he had
hired a hitman to kill his wife and then killed both of them himself.

The confession that followed stunned the city—and has Chicago
cops talking about the "ragged stranger" even today. Carl Wanderer was
sentenced to be hanged. He prefaced his execution with a horrible
rendition of a beloved religious song, to the chagrin of the gathered
crowd. Yet, despite his apparent deathbed conversion, and the swift
justice he was served, the ill will of Carl Wanderer is said to remain
unforgiven, as evidenced by the vengeful spirit of at least one of his
victims.

At the threshold of 4732 N. Campbell, neighbors report the sporadic
sighting of Ruth Wanderer, wandering the sidewalk. Others claim that
her horror is alive for all to *hear*. Wilson has heard rumors that the ghost
of Wanderer's wife still haunts the house and can occasionally be heard
screaming as if she had just realized that her husband was going to kill
her.

Yet, while unsuspecting victim Edward Masters went with Mrs.
Wanderer to the grave, presumably at the hand of the same killer, this
Lincoln Square street has not yet given up the ghost of the "ragged
stranger," a fact Wilson credits to the

bloody betrayal of a pregnant wife by her new husband, which
could have caused the anguished wife to haunt the place of her
death, or, more skeptically, could have caused people to imagine
her haunting the place of her murder.

Quite different were the circumstances surrounding the death of the
"ragged stranger" who, after all, only got what he was prepared to dish
out himself. Certainly, the justifiably killed do not usually return to
avenge their deaths, and so Masters may have gone in peace to his
questionable reward, without any desire to haunt his betrayer or his
Campbell Avenue neighbors.

Though the Wanderer haunting may seem incomplete to some, in
light of the missing ghost of Edward Masters, the force of the haunting
is unquestionable, as was the force of the original event on the future life

of Lincoln Square. As Wilson observes,

> For years the Campbell Avenue murders were the most widely-discussed and followed piece of gossip in the Lincoln Square neighborhood, but gradually the story shrank from people's consciousness as the decades passed and even more horrific crimes made the city newspapers. These murders would gradually have been forgotten in the years after they occurred, just another two of the thousands of murders that have plagued Chicago's history. What kept the story from disappearing altogether were the stories of Mrs. Wanderer's otherworldly cries—a ghost which keeps the neighborhood from forgetting a dark moment of its past.

An alternate name was used by request of the Lincoln Square resident who alerted the author to the reports of a Campbell Avenue haunting, leading the author to Ben Hecht's story of the "ragged stranger," which appears in Done in a Day: 100 Years of Great Writing *from* The Chicago Daily News. *An interesting aside to the story is found in this book, which recounts Hecht's visit to Wanderer just hours before the execution. During the visit, Hecht persuaded the doomed convict "to give a speech from the gallows in which he roundly and obscenely condemned the editors of the* Daily News. *Hecht had written the speech about his bosses and gave it to Wanderer, who put it in his pocket. Unfortunately, his jailers tied his hands behind him and he couldn't reach Hecht's speech, so he sang a religious song as the hood was placed over his head." One of the reporters present at the hanging reportedly remarked that, even if Wanderer was innocent of the crime, he deserved to be hanged for his voice. Ben Hecht's sketches of Chicago life are partially collected in* 1001 Afternoons in Chicago, *which includes a preface by editor Henry Justin Smith, from which Smith's quote is extracted.*

St. Ignatius Haunts

A likeness of Father Arnold Damen graces the
front yard of the school where his spirit lingers.

The Sacred Sentinel of a Grand Old School

ONE OF CHICAGO'S MOST enduring caches of paranormal lore is the Near South Side's complex of Holy Family Church and adjoining St. Ignatius College Preparatory High School, both of which have long been rumored to be watched over by pious sentinel Fr. Arnold Damen, founder of the nineteenth-century institutions. The preternatural episodes at the parish date back to at least 1871, when the devoted Damen, learning that Holy Family lay directly in the path of the Great Fire, instructed his parishioners to pray that the conflagration would circumvent the church. Miraculously, when the flames approached the massive structure, they suddenly detoured, cutting a path through adjoining neighborhoods and leaving Holy Family virtually untouched.

In thanksgiving for the divine intervention, parishioners erected a towering statue to Our Lady of Perpetual Help, who had saved their beloved church from the leveling conflagration. Visitors to the church during the twentieth century claimed to see faces in the plasterwork behind the statue; some have even photographed these curiosities.

But it is Damen himself and not the Divine who seems to have been, and continues to be, the center point around which the parish's fantastic occurrences have revolved, causing many to speculate about the true metaphysical power of this admittedly holy man. In the late nineteenth century, a pair of parish brothers, both altar servers, drowned together in a freak accident. Not long after, Damen was awoken by a vision of the boys, in their old servers' cassocks and bearing candles, who led him out of his rectory bed, across town, and into a run-down house where an old woman lay dying. Administering extreme unction, the last rites of the Roman Catholic Church, Damen returned, glassy-eyed, to his bed and sleep. In the morning, an errand boy rang the bell with news of a parishioner's death. During the previous night, the mother of the two dead brothers had suddenly died. Would a priest come quickly to pray over her body?

Of course, Damen already had.

But if Arnold Damen was always there for his church and his flock, protecting both from earthly, and netherworldly, harm, it was his beloved school that won his undying passion. St. Ignatius College Prep is an anomaly, a school unmatched for Chicago prestige, but open through scholarship to the super-rich, the dirt-poor, and everyone in between. The result is a student body that's an education in itself; those lucky and smart enough to gain admission live daily with a cross-section of society, forming friendships with young people from Hyde Park to Homewood, Bronzeville to Beverly, Garfield Park to the Gold Coast. St. Ignatius alums, then, are among the most sophisticated and successful of all Chicagoans. Fr. Damen would be proud. During his lifetime, the Jesuit strove for the school's superiority in all things: the curriculum, the culture, and, most notably, the spiritual life of the students it served. Some say that, after his death, Damen continued to serve as the school's headmaster of sorts, overseeing the campus in his usual, ever-loving way. Along with the well-being of the students, he keeps close watch on the physical property, ensuring that all is in tip-top shape and that Ignatius's future is secure.

When, in the early 1980s, the board initiated a massive renovation for the century-old school, elaborate plans were drawn up for the near-gutting of most of the structure, an updating of all the electrical and plumbing systems, and the installation of new floors and ceilings where water damage and wear had taken its toll. As with all such projects, a director was assigned to oversee the remodeling through to its completion. Not on the payroll, however, was another far more authoritative boss: Arnold Damen, the project's self-appointed foreman.

Since the founder's death, a number of students and faculty had spotted Damen casually patrolling the halls of Ignatius, going about his rounds as he always had, but by the dawn of the 1980s, sightings of him had all but ended. With the beginning of renovation Damen reappeared with a vengeance, startling those witnesses unschooled in his legacy.

One 1985 graduate tells the story of his own run-in with the ghost of Damen during an after-hours pledge drive for the renovation-in-progress:

In the mid-1980s, the school began a fundraising campaign to raise money for badly-needed repairs to the school. Some of the urgent work had already begun: replacing rotten flooring and tuckpointing. Students would work late into the night on this project, calling former students to raise money for the campaign.

The calling center was set up in an old, musty library on the top floor of the school, known then as the Cambridge Room. It was a dark and dreary place, with old, dusty books and sheets of plastic covering the windows. Outside employees who had been hired to manage the campaign often times worked late, too (past midnight), preparing letters and managing the records. They often felt strange sensations, like another person was in the room with them, when there were only two employees in the building. The school had a very sophisticated alarm system installed, since it was in a very bad area of the city, and several times this alarm went off while the fundraising campaign was being conducted— the keypad had an LCD display that would ominously flash the word "Intruder" when the alarm went off. Though the system had been in place for several years it had never before experienced a false alarm, so every time the alarm would go off the Chicago police would respond with canine teams, and the school would be searched, with negative results. There were never any indications of forcible entry, and everything was always found locked and secured.

One night, I was standing in the library talking to one of the management people, when I glanced through the set of large, old wooden doors that led to an unused hallway. The hallway also served as a foyer for two old curved stairways, an old elevator, and a large storeroom. I watched an old man about five-foot, six-inches tall and very thin, with white hair, balding, extremely pale, and dressed all in black clothing (a long-sleeved black shirt and long slacks). The person moved very quickly and lightly on a diagonal across the wide hallway, and it was odd, since the floors were very old wood and creaked badly; even so, no sound was made by this man I saw.

I said to the manager, *There is someone in the building*, and I pointed out to the hallway and told him what I'd seen. He told the other manager, and they were concerned and went to investigate. As the stairwell was closed off and the elevators not in service, the only place the old man could have gone was into the storeroom on the south side of the hallway. The room was, surprisingly, locked, and when the manager unlocked the door, we found that the floor and ceiling of the room had already been removed by construction crews working on the renovations. We looked down nearly twenty feet to the classroom below and up nearly twenty feet into the pitch black ceiling of the attic of the school.

We were terrified. A hasty meeting was called and the students were sent home several hours early. The managers—who had, of course, had their own experiences in the building—left with us, and no one was willing to look through the upper floors of the school that night, or to call the police, who had come in vain more than once before to apprehend "intruders" who couldn't be found.

Later, when I told older priests at the school what I'd seen, there was no question in their minds that I'd seen Fr. Damen, the founder of the school, to whom the physical maintenance of the building had always been of the utmost importance. Although I knew well of Damen, as he occupied the most prominent of places in the school's proud history, I had never heard the stories of his haunting of the place. Still, everyone I spoke to who knew of the priest's ghost asserted at once that he had likely come back—as he had many times before—this time to keep an eye on the renovations.

The story of Fr. Arnold Damen was told to the author by an anonymous graduate of St. Ignatius in the fall of 1998.

WAUCONDA HAUNTS

Photo by Bruce Nicholson.

This farmhouse kitchen has served up a
number of remarkable visual apparitions.

Clairvoyant Encounters
with Lake County's Past

MOST GHOSTHUNTERS FACE great difficulties in performing their duties. With no manifest psychic abilities to point them toward the phantoms in question, they are left with only the tools of accepted science: electromagnetic field meters, thermal guns, night vision goggles, parabolic microphones. Yet, no matter how sensitive their equipment is, it can tell little about what's really going on. Even if impressive and unexplainable environmental fluctuations do occur, their origins remain a mystery. Little satisfaction for those trying to discern the truly disembodied.

Clairvoyant ghosthunters, then, have the distinct upper hand, even if their results, often astounding and quite revealing, are, for the most part, rejected by our scientific paradigm. The gift, or skill, of seeing psychic objects and events (those invisible to the normal human eye) is a rare one. Clairvoyants can at times visit a murder scene and see the tragedy replayed, thereafter leading police to the killer. Others can hold in their hand a missing person's house keys and receive a mental picture of where their owner is. Still others may attend a church service and witness angelic beings gathering around the altar as the program progresses. Yet others are blessed, or cursed, with the seeing of ghosts.

Bruce Nicholson is a Des Plaines mail carrier who, in recent years, has developed his own clairvoyance, an aptitude which assists him in some most unusual projects. By using his photography skills and clairvoyant abilities, Nicholson tries to help people with their paranormal problems. One such problem was presented by a man on his postal route: John R. Roney, who owns a farmhouse in the town of Wauconda on the estate where his ancestors settled many generations ago. Here, Nicholson tells the proud history of the farm and its inhabitants, and the steps he took in searching for its spirits:

There are a few remaining farmhouses in Lake County, Illinois, waiting to be torn down, due to modernization and property values. Right on the outskirts of Wauconda Township (which is known for its apple orchard and resort lake) lies a vacant farm estate with over one-and-one-half centuries worth of history, between the farm property and its past inhabitants. Unfortunately, the farm buildings are scheduled to be demolished and replaced by newer homes.

As mentioned above, the farm estate, originally owned by a John Roney (Sr.), had been documented in the Lake County records for the following: In 1839 the original land deed was signed by President Andrew Jackson, and in 1845 the same Wauconda farm had the distinction of being the first site in Lake County on which a frame house was built.

In addition to the brief farm land history, the Roney family had made its mark on local history as some of the earliest settlers. The Wauconda chapter of Roneys started in 1836 when John Roney (Sr.) of County Down, Ireland, wed Ann Kendall of London, England, in the town of Pittsburgh, Pennsylvania. Three years later, Mr. and Mrs. Roney moved westward into Illinois where they became permanent residents.

During Ann's childbearing years, she had given birth to four daughters and one son. John, Sr. provided income to support his wife and children through his many real estate investments. He actually owned eighty acres of land where the Chicago Stock Yards used to be. Once grown up, all four daughters married into prominent families, leaving the only son born to carry on the Roney name.

John F. Roney was born in 1845 on the Wauconda farm. Nineteen years later, he bought a section of his dad's farm property. John F. was the person responsible for building the farmhouse which still stands today. Then, Mr. J.F. Roney met a Margaret McDonald, whom he married seven years later.

Together, Mr. and Mrs. J.F. Roney parented ten children. John F.'s means of income were split between business and farming. At this point, the Roneys were known around Lake County for the distribution of fine dairy goods to grocery stores. John also had other income from raising livestock.

As years passed on, the original Roney clan either died or moved out of the Wauconda area. The family-owned business had begun to dwindle, leaving the farm as a summer vacation home. Shortly afterwards, the farmhouse had to be vacated because of extensive water damage.

Afterwards, one of the Roney descendants, a great-grandson named John R. Roney, along with a groundskeeper named Lenny, tried to keep the estate house and grounds. John R. had many fond memories of his childhood at the farm. Evidently, the farm had plenty of memories, too, for other relatives still reside there in spirit form.

John and Lenny had suspected that the farmhouse harbored ghosts ever since they both heard footsteps upstairs and doors closing by themselves without any physical explanations. John was searching for answers to why this paranormal activity was taking place. This was when and why he decided to ask me for help.

The first time I visited the Roney farm estate was on February 25, 2000. It was an unusually warm, foggy morning, and my daughter, Jennifer, joined me. Together we drove till we found a narrow opening off to the side of the road. There were two stone pillars separating the dirt road. Posted was a NO TRESPASSING sign. We continued down the back road surrounded on each side by tall trees. It resembled a scene from *Wuthering Heights*. Upon reaching our destination, we walked past an iron gate covered in vines. There in the background stood the three-story farm mansion.

John greeted us at the door. He then gave us a minor tour of the main floor of the house. There was literally no furniture to sit on, so Jennifer and I stood there listening to John tell us about his ancestors. Actually, Mr. Roney had an interesting story to tell us, involving his uncle and two aunts.

John's Aunt Marion had died at age 17 of rheumatic fever. Her brother, Arthur, had such a brotherly love for her that he actually carried the deathly ill Marion in his arms to the high school graduation to receive her diploma. Four weeks afterward, she passed away. Then another tragedy struck. Arthur accidentally broke his neck while diving in Lake Michigan. Shortly after his death, another aunt named Genevieve noticed Arthur's face in one of the farmhouse windows.

When we had finished talking with John, he told us to make

ourselves at home while he wandered off for some coffee in the next town.

Though the atmosphere of the place—and our aloneness—were daunting, neither was going to stop us from our exploration. I had begun to search each room, with my daughter close behind. What I was trying to check for were energies that spirits emit, commonly called hot and cold spots. It seemed like energy was moving throughout the mansion. I had found that the highest concentration of energy was always in the kitchen, and fifty percent of all the photos I eventually took were taken there. Afterward, John showed up with coffee for everyone. Before leaving, we thanked him. I took two photos of the kitchen from the outside. This concluded the first visit.

Later that evening I brought my film into a one-hour photo shop to be developed. I prefer this because the regular photo labs tend to alter any unusual images obtained, thinking them to be flaws. I never had a chance to pick up the photographs until the next day, but when I did, I found some amazing results.

I had caught one female presence standing next to a broom in the living room where part of the ceiling had fallen in. Another photograph showed a hooded face and two more female apparitions dressed in Victorian-style wardrobe. All three entities had been looking out the kitchen window at me.

This was the proof I needed.

The second time I visited the Roney mansion—in March—I brought a small group of ten people with me. They consisted of friends and clairvoyants, some of them both. John Roney was acting as a tour guide for us and proceeded to lecture us on his ancestors as the group followed him room by room. John and the ten guests were so loud I thought they would wake up the dead. It became too difficult to sense any paranormal activity, so I had immediately exited to the kitchen. There I again picked up strong vibrations, and there was also a green mist present. I shot my camera twice, capturing the energy form of an apparition. By this time, John and others were downstairs. Mr. Roney said his good-byes and told me to lock up the place when we were done.

This was when things started happening.

My wife, Kim, had seen a dark shadow race by in her peripheral vision. Another friend named Janie had felt pressure on her shoulders, like someone was eavesdropping on our conversation. Before leaving the house, everyone present heard an animal scamper over the living room ceiling, followed by light human footfalls. Three of the men in the group ran upstairs. I grabbed a fire poker, because I had seen how mean raccoons can be. We were upstairs in the room where the noise had come from, but there was no evidence of people or animals. This ended the second visit.

The final tour took place in June. There were twenty-one people entering Mr. Roney's farmhouse late at night. Despite the large number of people present, we had several photos taken with images in them. In addition to the pictures, one girl on the tour had her long hair gently stroked from behind. At this time we decided to leave the mansion or risk being eaten alive by giant mosquitoes.

The evidence found in the Roney farmhouse is as follows: I have taken many photos of female presences inside the house. There were two photos of a thin woman in her thirties. This woman was caught on film each time near the falling ceiling. She may have been one of the original owners that didn't like her house in such disarray.

I also captured in a photo frame two women and a hooded face. One can see that the girl in the middle is a teenager, possibly close to Marion's age, and in one of the group portraits of the Roney family, I saw an enormous aura around Marion's head. Another entity could be Arthur, as illustrated by the photograph I took at the house which contained an energy form of an apparition; this particular entity had something wrong with his neck. Aunt Genevieve's claim that she had seen Arthur's face in the farmhouse window after his death backs up the possibility that his spirit is still there.

I do believe that the John R. Roney farm estate is haunted by Marion and Arthur, who both both died elsewhere but came back to reunite as sister and brother in the tranquil setting of the farmhouse.

Besides these two, there are several other unidentifiable entities that are displaced in and around the Roney mansion.

None of these seem harmful, just sadfully lost.

Bruce Nicholson followed up a telephone conversation with the author with a detailed account of his visits to the Roney farm in a written letter to the author in the summer of 2000.

OVALTINE HAUNTS

Photo by D. Cowan.

The once weed-choked entry gate has been cleared at last for
the revitalization of this beloved west suburban landmark.

Devilish Deeds Taint Villa Park's Malted Memories

THESE DAYS, NO SELF-RESPECTING spirit would be caught, well, dead at the old Ovaltine factory in west suburban Villa Park. The massive complex, built in 1917 by the Wander Company of Switzerland, is on its way to new splendor as the site of a 300+ unit residential development, complete with swimming pool, fitness center, and a wealth of other amenities. These days, the few buildings that remain here are abuzz with life, their windows sealed against dust and ne'er-do-wells, the surrounding paths cleared of overgrowth and planted and repaved in anticipation of strollers and joggers. The project, as unwelcome as it may be to those aching from gentrification, is a big improvement over the Ovaltine of the past decade and a half. The renovation marks the end to a neighborhood's nightmare, which began when the plant's closing in 1985 opened the door to a reign of fear and frustration, an era that began with the breaking of the factory windows.

When the first of the Ovaltine buildings were built, its owners hoped to bring their most prominent European product, a malted milk drink powder, to consumers in the United States. After nearly 70 years of astounding success, including the building of a post office to handle the nonstop requests for Little Orphan Annie premiums, the original plant was shut down and the operation moved to sleek new digs in Minneapolis. For 14 years thereafter, 23 buildings were sitting ducks for squatters, vandals, drug dealers, firebugs, and a nasty dose of amateur occultists. While arguments raged among would-be developers, historical preservationists, zoning officials, and tax collectors, dark intruders claimed the mammoth hollow that waited in the middle of it all. Frequent fires were set by the homeless, who slept in offices next to huge factory rooms where alleged devil worshippers performed their weekend rituals. In time, the upper floors of the buildings grew foreboding, their dirty and broken windows framing fires that burned throughout the night. During the 14 years of abandonment, hundreds of arrests were made on the 15-acre site.

As the public war proceeded, locals fought a private battle with a largely unknown enemy, calling in reports of bonfires, blaring music, ghastly screams, and graffiti that led to futile searches of the labyrinthine property and the swift return of the culprits after the police left.

Despite the grim reality, some thought the rumors were worse. Neighborhoods kids would return from Saturday night forays into the factory with incredible stories. Some described voices and cries that came from nowhere, voices that knew their names. Others claimed that the place was charged with an unnatural energy, and that debris from big piles had been thrown violently into them, unaided by human hands.

After the dark days between 1985 and 1998, it seemed that even Captain Midnight couldn't save Ovaltine from once-protective Villa Park residents who, after more than enough trouble, changed their hopes for preservation into a vow to raze the place. When, in December of 1997, the remains of the plant were finally sold for residential development, locals credited a miracle and looked to the day when the curse would be lifted from Annie's kingdom.

Though drywall and can lighting lie on Ovaltine's horizon, something may remain here that isn't in the floor plans. For while the witches and wanderers are gone now, stories are still told of the things that remain and, in the days ahead, residents may wonder about the voices and mysterious events infesting their Ovaltine apartments.

Meanwhile, people living in the neighborhood surrounding the development will likely continue to be haunted by a much more stubborn spirit: the memory of life here during Ovaltine's 70-year heyday.

As one resident mourned, *It was such a happy time here. Now the whole thing is just sad.*

Background information on Ovaltine was provided by "Villa Park cringes over delay in tearing down Ovaltine: leaders hope lawsuit means eyesore will soon be thing of past." (DuPage County Daily Herald, *Saturday, May 24, 1997, p. 6/sec. 6). Oral reports of activity at abandoned Ovaltine were furnished by anonymous suburban residents on a number of occasions.*

Guardian Haunts

Keeping a Hand In

SIXTEEN-YEAR-OLD **P**ALATINE RESIDENT **I**SABELLE Burtan
spent the first half of her life in Chicago. The daughter of caterers, she
became acclimated to babysitters early on; most mornings when she
awoke, both Mom and Dad were long gone, Isabelle left in the capable
hands of live-in caregivers. When, in 1991, a particularly beloved
babysitter left her longtime position with the Burtans, seven-year-old
Isabelle was devastated at the loss. She would soon discover, however,
that another entity was ready to fill the void with a most bizarre
presence:

> My parents have always gone to work around 2 A.M., so when I
> was a little kid, they'd hire nannies; more like live-in housekeepers
> that would take care of me in the mornings, and then clean the
> house a little and cook dinner before they would return at two in
> the afternoon.
>
> One of these nannies was a cousin of mine from Poland named
> Dorothy. She was with us for four years, and since I'd known her
> since age three, she was another member of the family to me,
> something like a second mother.
>
> My parents and I went on a cruise over Christmas break when
> I was seven, and when we returned, Dorothy was gone—no good-
> bye or anything. My parents knew that she was going to be
> leaving, but I had no clue whatsoever.
>
> That night, the night we had returned to find her gone, my mom
> decided she'd miss work the next day to stay with me in the morn-
> ing. As we all settled down to sleep, me in my bedroom, my par-
> ents in theirs, I started crying into my pillow.
>
> My mom had made me a sort of tent around my bed, so that
> when I laid back on my pillow, there was the top to a circus tent
> hanging above me, filled with pockets overflowing with stuffed

animals and toys. I didn't want my parents to know that I was crying, because I blamed them for Dorothy's leaving, and I untied two little bows that held back a curtain that hung from the tent, completely covering the head of my bed. I fell asleep quickly and completely forgot to turn on my nightlight (a necessity at the time).

I woke up in the middle of the night after hearing a noise. I can't remember what the noise was, where it came from or anything. I just remember being surprised awake. I immediately said the name *Dorothy* . . . thinking she would be asleep in a pull-out bed by mine like she had for four years. I heard someone whisper something back, something barely audible, but it definitely resembled a human whisper, enough for a seven-year-old to assume it was her nanny. I don't know what the person was saying, though, and still don't know what it could've been.

It didn't hit me she was gone until I parted the curtains and peered into the room, to see if I had woken her up. I remember feeling very cold because I curled up my whole body to squeeze inside the little tent and pulled all the covers in to comfort me— which could mean nothing since it was Chicago in mid-winter, and though our heating was good, the window was less than a foot away from my bed.

When I saw that there was no bed, no person in the room, I remember freezing, mortified. I didn't want to close the curtains because I was sure the whisper would come back and, convinced that a burglar had just been in the room or something, I wanted to run to my parents' room.

Before I could, however, this hand appeared in front of my face. I don't know how else to describe it. It looked like the open palm of a hand. It was floating right in front of my face, just outside the curtains, and it didn't seem real or like something I could touch, but it was there. It was clear and smoky at the same time . . . not like some ghostly thing, but more like a strange foggy object that seemed to be very bright yet very dark at once. I know I'm not making much sense, but that's about as well as I can describe this thing I saw.

I remember pinching myself then, because Dorothy had always told me to pinch myself if I was having a nightmare or a strange dream. The pinch didn't jolt me awake. I had been awake the whole time.

I sat frozen. This hand thing didn't make any movement, it was just there.

I don't know how long I just looked at it. I wasn't afraid of it; I wasn't even startled by it being there. I just saw it and registered what I saw, completely fascinated more than anything.

Finally, I remember lying back onto my pillow, thinking the hand would leave. I seemed much more calm and sleepy than I had before and didn't even mind if it stayed there.

I finally closed my eyes to go to sleep, but I could still see the hand, only in negative format, like when you look at a bright light and then close your eyes, you see the light's reverse shadow. And now I was getting annoyed, because the hand was making me calm, but wouldn't leave me alone. So I opened my eyes and started thinking, *go away*, really hard, probably for fifteen minutes, though it seemed like hours. Now I was getting really upset, because it didn't leave.

I was just about to turn around onto my stomach, as if to ignore it, when it started moving. It started making a sort of stretching motion with what would be fingertips, and would come closer towards me, almost touching me, and then pulling away with a closed palm. This continued a couple of times, and I remember shaking my head and protesting to it doing this. I tried to look to the side and away from it, but no matter where I looked, I knew it was there. Finally, I started crying because I didn't understand what was going on, and as suddenly as it had appeared, the hand went away.

I was so happy to be rid of it, I fell fast asleep and thought not much more of it until I got much older and realized that seeing a floating hand was not an average childhood experience.

The hand reappeared to me the night we moved into my new house, when I was nine years old. That first night, I remember falling asleep feeling happy and content, not nervous or sad in any way. I woke up very early that morning, maybe around 4:30 A.M., and I remember just sitting in my room, visualizing what a new life in Palatine would be like. And then I remember it hitting me that I was gone away from the hand. For whatever reason, though I hadn't though about my experience in at least two years, I was suddenly glad to have moved far away from it. I fell back asleep feeling very relieved.

I woke again at around 9:30 A.M. and I looked at the clock at my bedside to see how long I had slept. It was broad daylight, and my bedroom window has an eastern exposure. The room fairly glowed from the sunlight and the brand new whitewash reflected so much light I had to squint a few times as I looked up at the ceiling. And there was the hand again.

This time it looked more like two hands with arms, too. The strange haze looked the same as I had seen it before, but this time the arms were moving, kind of going back and forth, towards me and away from me, first one then the other. This time, I was petrified, it dawning on me that this was strange and this was a new house. I couldn't move, and just stared as hard as I could at the foggy hand-things, praying that they would disappear.

They finally did, vanishing in a split second, and when I glanced back at the clock it was around 10:15 A.M., and I could hear my parents waking up and moving around in the room next to mine.

Isabelle Burtan shared her recollection of the vision of hands with the author in a written account in the winter of 2000.

CUBA ROAD HAUNTS

Author's photo.

This tiny, suburban burial ground is closely
tied to the folklore of the road outside.

Road to No One

WHITE CEMETERY HAS BEEN striking terror into the hearts of north suburban teenagers for as long as this eerie boneyard has lain here in the sparsely populated region near Barrington, Illinois. The acreage sprawls modestly just east of the highway called Old Barrington, and some say that this relatively ancient graveyard, circa 1820, is the cause of the neighborhood's very bad reputation.

The bizarre phenomena of White Cemetery are immeasurable. A vast array of wonders has been reported by visitors to this site, including the sound of leaves crunching under invisible feet and tombstones toppling for no apparent reason. Most common is the sighting of white orbs of light that linger over tombstones before floating off into the night. Sometimes, these shimmering balls are accompanied by luminescent figures that ease in and out of the cemetery through the iron fence, sending frightened witnesses to the local authorities to report UFOs and extraterrestrial visitors. Local teens have a different, more traditional take on the White Cemetery phenomena. The lights and shadows, they say, are just a few of the many phantoms of Cuba Road.

For Chicagoland ghosthunters, Cuba Road is the single most notorious haunted site north of southwest suburban Bachelors Grove Cemetery. In fact, the road shares not only the intensity of Bachelors Grove, but many of the same phenomena. Along with flashing lights and phantom cars that echo those reported at the Grove, this is the land of the other "magic house," one of two in the Chicagoland area that appear and disappear as baffled witnesses look on. Like its sister house nestled (sometimes) in the woodland path to Bachelors Grove, the house on Cuba Road is said to have actually existed at some point in the past. While the fate of the Bachelors Grove house is not known, however, locals insist that the house on Cuba Road burned to the ground in a mysterious fire.

Cuba Road's so-called ghost house has at least one occupant, according to eyewitnesses who have seen her: an old woman who wanders the road outside the spot where the house has been seen. Whoever this woman is, she is not alone on Cuba; translucent cars piloted by invisible drivers motor past, sometimes turning into White Cemetery and disappearing. On summer nights, a mysterious couple walks arm and arm along the deserted stretch of roadway, vanishing into the horizon.

Most compelling of all the Cuba Road tales is the one tied by Arlington Heights historian Bev Ottaviano to the gangster era, when Chicago hoodlums would grab some R&R in the lake-studded regions surrounding Barrington and Lake Zurich. In those good old days, the free-wheeling, fun-loving goodfellas descended on the sleepy towns, fishing and sunning with the rest of the 9-to-5 world, though their dinner attire was, perhaps, a bit flashier. But gangsters they were, and fear coursed through these towns when the boys from Chicago came up to play. Some of that unease lingers in the story that warns of a cigar-chomping Mafioso who appears in the rear-view mirror of drivers turning on to Cuba Road. The specific identity of the passenger remains unknown, but his occupation is apparent.

Though Cuba Road is the star of every north suburban fright night, another minor highway has lately been featured. Rainbow Road, which intersects Cuba, boasts a classic haunted house, complete with gossip: the decaying mansion, locked behind an iron fence, is rumored to have been a notorious sanitarium. Many a fun-loving teenager has gotten more than he bargained for in snooping around this off-limits site. A group of Fremd High Schoolers drove along Rainbow one night with the intention of breaking into the crumbling estate but, as they were rattling the gates, attempting to shake loose the rusted lock, they heard a sound like a baseball bat smashing into something. Racing back to their car, they found a huge dent in the side. Another team of pranksters?

Perhaps.

Still, this lively assortment of phenomena has been luring suburban teenagers to Cuba Road and Rainbow Road for decades, inspiring all manner of dares and double-dares. Those up to the challenge often reap rewards in the form of unshakable chills and timeless stories for their grandchildren. One Fremd student, a veteran Cuba Road adventurer, remembers her own initiation into the wonders of White Cemetery.

We were fooling around—like typical teenagers—when I was dared to run around this tree that was about fifty feet from the car and come back. I am so freaked out about things like that but I did it. As I was running back to the car I stubbed my foot right into a gravestone. That night, not long after, we went back to that grave, and against the grave was a wooden cane leaning against the headstone around where my foot hit it.

Unbelievable? Maybe. But a classmate and a thousand other witnesses yet believe:

One night I was driving past the cemetery and I saw police lights, blue and red, flashing over the hill not more than 200 yards ahead of me. When I reached the top . . . nothing. Not a car in sight and everything as calm and still as could be.

No one on the road but me.

Arlington Heights historian Bev Ottaviano furnished the author with the background history and folklore of Cuba Road and White Cemetery. Supporting personal accounts were drawn from letters of Fremd High School students sent to the author in the spring of 2000.

Montrose Point Haunts

Author's photo.

Gently-worn footpaths meander past the enigmatic "Magic Hedge."

Into the Magic Hedge

LIKE THE REST OF Lincoln Park, the section of public lakefront area sprawling between Waveland and Montrose Avenues has become a popular recreational area, both for residents of the adjacent Lakeview and Buena Park neighborhoods and for those that come there on nice days by foot, car, bike, or rollerblade, many for tennis or golf or for softball games at the Waveland Avenue facilities, fewer to catch sight of the strays that wander from the city's bird sanctuary in the woods beyond the ball field.

With its sparsely used beach, a rarity along the lakefront's endless miles, Montrose Point serves its own free spirits, many of them Hispanic-Americans from nearby Uptown who transform the wide lawns of the Montrose Harbor area into soccer fields, and retirees who fish off the pier from early morning to nighttime.

But all has not always been fun and games here.

Shortly after World War II, the Chicago Park District leased Montrose Point to the United States Army for one dollar a year, so the latter might develop a military post to watch for Russian invasions. The Army first established a gunsite, then replaced it with a Nike missile site. Nearly 300 men were stationed here, with barracks, a mess hall, a radar station, officers' quarters, and other facilities.

As with any military base, the staff of Montrose Point came from all over the country. As with any such situation, most of the servicemen got along. At times, however, tempers flared. And sometimes, they stayed that way, arguments leading to clashes, fists, and worse. James Landing, a professor at the University of Illinois at Chicago, tells a story of these Cold War times at Montrose and the lake:

> According to eyewitness accounts, of which there are only a few left, one Halloween evening two soldiers got into a heated

argument. One was a young European immigrant from Massachusetts named Pique Nerjee, and the other was a southern cotton farm worker born in Puerto Rico named Hernando Cortez Rodrickkez. The argument became so heated that Rodrickkez threatened to kill Pique. Pique remained in the barracks afterward, since he was on duty that night, but Hernando left the barracks at about 9 P.M., since he had been invited to a masked ball and Halloween party at the national office of the W.C.T.U. in Evanston. Based on later Army reports, a strange noise was heard in the barracks around 12 A.M., enough to cause the men to get up and look around. It was only later that they noticed that Pique did not rise, and when they checked, he appeared dead.

When the coroner arrived to investigate, suddenly Hernando rushed into the barracks shouting, *Pique, Pique, please Pique*. It seemed that Hernando had heard the same noise at the party and, like a man obsessed, told everyone that he had to return to his post immediately. After they took Pique's body away, Hernando ran out of the barracks, moaning and wailing, *Pique, Pique, please Pique*.

The soldiers followed, but the night had become misty and fogged and, had it not been for a full moon, they would have seen nothing. Although they heard the moaning and wailing all night, they could not find Hernando, and he was, in fact, never seen again. The Army pronounced him dead (he was believed to have jumped into the freezing autumn waters of Lake Michigan) and reported Pique dead of a sudden heart attack.

The incident was soon forgotten but, the following Halloween night, soldiers in the barracks saw strange figures walking through the shrubs along the barracks (the area known today as "The Magic Hedge"), grabbed their rifles and tried to intercept the intruders.

Nothing!

Each time they returned to the barracks, the strange figures began moving through the shrubs. One time they listened carefully and heard a low moan and wail that sounded something like, *Pique, Pique, please Pique*, and that is what was reported to their commanding officer.

By the next Halloween the Nike missile site had been removed, but two homeless men sleeping in the park told police that all night "vampire bats" had kept attacking them, whispering that they wanted to suck their blood. Birders dismissed these stories, concluding that the so-called vampire bats were probably owls, and that the wails and moans were the shrieking of the prey they caught, like rabbits and rats.

And so the explanation went—until about five years ago, when some construction workers at Montrose, doing emergency night sewer work, were distracted by a strange light running through the Magic Hedge. They checked but found nothing more, although they did report a low moaning and wailing of words that they described to their superiors as *Pique, Pique, please Pique.*

James Landing provided the story of Montrose Point in a written account to the author in the spring of 1999.

CHRISTIANA STREET HAUNTS

Boyhood Haunts of
a Magickal Monk

INNUMERABLE ARE THE TALES of vengeful ghosts remaining—or returning—to right the wrongs done them in life. Certainly, if we are to believe the stories, the misdeeds of the living are often repaid with a lifetime of haunting, much to the horror of the unsuspecting survivors.

Rare, though, are accounts of spirits who, having wronged others in life, return at death for another shot at the object of their disaffection. Yet, such hard-hearted and cold-blooded souls do seem to exist, living out their sad lives embittered by grudges and spending their afterlives trying to get in a last, angry word. That is, if their mortal enemies let them.

Reverend Julian von Duerbeck knows from malevolent spirits. A priest and monk of St. Procopius Abbey, situated in west suburban Lisle, von Duerbeck is far from a retiring rural friar—indeed, no less than a nobleman; his family received a grant of Imperial Nobility in 1590 for loyalty to Rodolf von Hapsburg of Austria and Sigismond Bathory of Transylvania (yes, Transylvania). In addition to the inherited distinctions, Fr. Julian has added his own impressive titles to the family name; he is a Knight of the Company of the Rose, a member of the Monastic Interreligious Dialogue, and Adjunct Professor of History of Religion at Benedictine University. In addition, von Duerbeck has appeared a number of times on CNN and on A&E to discuss occult topics, in which he is more than amply schooled.

Ancestral and intellectual triumphs notwithstanding, von Duerbeck started out as a Chicago kid, raised in the North Side niche of Old Irving Park. And, in fact, it was right here in the old neighborhood that Julian garnered some of his most intimate knowledge of the ethereal, growing up in the area's reputedly haunted house. Yet, though Julian and his family experienced firsthand some of the chilling events that made the place's reputation, none was more disturbing than von Duerbeck's teenaged run-in there with a decidedly non-resident wraith: a deliberately estranged relative who, after years of self-imposed exile, tried to pay a last call on her much-maligned relations:

We moved into that house in 1959 and left in 1970. According to neighborhood stories, that house was haunted since World War II, when an old man committed suicide in the "English basement." Five different members of my family found the atmosphere of the basement oppressive during the hours of 3:30 to 5:30 P.M. Three relatives left the basement a number of times after feeling someone behind them. Once, it took five people to open the door, because it kept being pushed back, though no one was inside. The front entrance was a locked room with a dirt floor and a cross on the wall; the room above (the actual entrance to the house) we called "The Cold Room." It exhibited that psychic and physical coldness often connected with hauntings.

Despite my Transylvanian ancestry and my family's love of Halloween, no member of my family has entered that house or basement since 1970.

My father and mother were distant cousins, my father's branch becoming Lutheran, my mother's staying Catholic. My father did convert to Catholicism before marriage, and one of his aunts, Emma, resented my mother because of his decision.

At a party at my grandmother's house, my mother (pregnant with me) stepped up to Emma to kiss her. Emma thrust my mother down the stairs, and my father saved us by leaping forward in time. The party was ruined, of course, and my grandmother was furious with her sister. Emma thereafter stayed away from the family, choosing to live in Florida.

Fifteen years later, my mother and I were talking in the kitchen in our house on Christiana Street in Chicago's Irving Park neighborhood. Suddenly, my Boston Terrier fled the room, and we heard a sound on the porch. As I approached the door, we saw the doorknob turning, and we both were filled with a crushing sense of dread and impending danger. My mother called out,

Don't touch it.

I went to the far window overseeing the porch, and while we

both watched the doorknob turn, I saw that no one was on the porch. Then it stopped, and the sense of danger left us.

A couple of hours later, we heard my father's usual steps up the stairs. As he entered with his key, my mother said, *Joe, the strangest thing happened today.*

My father interrupted, saying, *Wait, Fran, I have to tell you. My sister Marie called. Emma died two hours ago.*

Was the visiting a last blast of psychic hatred to the two people in danger years before? What would have happened if I had opened the door? Many years later, I offered a Mass for the repose of Emma's soul.

Fr. Julian von Duerbeck provided the author a written account of his family's experiences in summer 2000.

KRAFT FOODS HAUNTS

Author's photo.

Builders of this corporate fortress have some wild stories to tell.

Northfield's Unsavory Excavation

WELL **KNOWN TO FANS OF** the 1980s movie blockbuster, *Poltergeist,* is the trouble that comes when burial grounds are disturbed. Chicagoland residents are particularly in tune with this phenomenon. After the old City Cemetery was relocated, the bodies re-interred at points north of the city, builders on the old land were surprised to find human remains as they dug the foundations for their new houses. Those who disrespectfully disposed of these remains found themselves, in many cases, living with uninvited houseguests.

Untold numbers of Chicago-area residents also live near ancient Indian cemeteries and tribal sites, many of them containing the graves of unfriendly natives, hostile in life to white encroachment. For many years, developers wisely shied away from building directly on these spots. If any additions were made, they were usually in the form of graves, when Native-American burial sites were converted into Anglo ones.

In recent decades, however, as property costs soared and desirable land became scarcer, sensibilities began to give way. The resulting developments, subdivisions sprawling over sacred grounds, were often ill-fated. Witness the infamous case of Deanna Gallo, whose Orland Hills home was, in the early 1980s, plagued by flames shooting out of the wall sockets. When baffled firefighters shut off the house's electric in order to trace the problem, the phenomena continued, leading some researchers to believe that Gallo, an adolescent, may well have been a poltergeist agent, a channel through which energy, either from her own body or an external source, manifested itself. Those who believed an external energy responsible for the "haunting" of Deanna speculated that her suburban home had been built on an old Native-American cemetery, guessing that Gallo was acting as an outlet of sorts for the outraged energy of the disturbed Indians.

Human remains are not the only ones that fuss when their resting places are disturbed in the name of progress. In north suburban Northfield, the building of a new plant for Kraft Foods came at the cost of the typical headaches and a few highly unexpected ones.

The construction site had formerly housed the old Techny Seminary, property of the Divine Word Monastery. A number of the school's buildings had been left behind for future use, along with a few other permanent fixtures. When work on Kraft began, a group of unexplained headstones on the property was fenced off to protect them from accidental harm. Yet, an unexpected excavation would suggest that developers had not been careful enough, that more mysterious burials had taken place on the site of this future corporate park. One worker recalls the bizarre discovery, and the even stranger events that followed:

> When the Gulf War started, there was a massive airlift of equip-
> ment from Glenview Naval Air Station, and the flight pattern was
> directly overhead of this very large construction site. Some of the
> men on the job wondered about these head stones that were fenced
> off to protect the area where they had been placed. Then, during
> the excavation for the basements and ice vaults of the new plant,
> the remains of horses were unearthed.

> About a year and a half later, just about when the job was to
> be turned over, rumors arose among the temporary security people
> and some of the remaining construction workers that, on a number
> of occasions, the sound of horses had been heard in the building,
> the sound as of a team of them galloping through the halls.

Information on the Techny property was provided by the Divine Word Foundation. The account of the unearthing at the Kraft site was provided by an anonymous worker in a written account to the author in the summer of 2000.

WASHINGTON BOULEVARD HAUNTS

Photo courtesy of the Chicago Public Library.

At the armory near the disaster site, fretful relations and friends thread through the maze of bodies after the capsizing of the *Eastland*.

The Eastland Goes On

ONE OF CHICAGO'S MOST secret hauntings is, ironically, also one of its most famous: the reported paranormality of Oprah Winfrey's Harpo Studios. A number of years ago, Oprah herself is reported to have admitted to experiencing bizarre goings-on at Harpo, which is housed in the old Armory on Washington Boulevard. Though the details of the Harpo ghosts are, like all of Winfrey's business, off-limits to the public, interest in the tales remains high.

The haunting of Harpo is popularly supposed to stem from the use of the building as a temporary morgue in the summer of 1915, when the *Eastland* steamer capsized in the Chicago River, a mammoth tragedy that ended with the burial of more than 800 bodies, including nearly two dozen families, who had been on board for a weekend picnic cruise to Michigan City, Indiana. The cheerful chaos of the departure preparations quickly gave way to pure horror when the docked steamer suddenly tipped over, drowning dozens of passengers and trapping hundreds below deck, where they had sought early shelter from a morning drizzle. Rescue workers and regular citizens spent the long afternoon at grisly tasks: pulling body after body from the waterlogged vessel and dragging the river for stray corpses. By early evening, the floor of the Armory was lined with nearly 500 of *Eastland*'s victims.

A few days passed before strollers on the Clark Street bridge began reporting phantom screams and pleas coming from the dark water where the tragedy had played out and, in the ensuing years, whispers arose, too, about the lingering of souls at the old Washington Boulevard Armory.

A former copywriter at an advertising agency located at Washington Boulevard and Aberdeen Street reports that the *Eastland* victims may not only linger, but wander. Coworkers who remain at the agency confirm that something seems to share their workspace, a building that snuggles right up to the former Armory. Though the worker had heard reports of strange activity from the time she joined the agency, she was hardly convinced that something truly paranormal was to blame

... until it happened to me. My first experience happened in the fall of 1998. I was in very early one weekend morning, working on a catalog with two other women. We were each in our respective offices, on opposite corners of the floor, and we were the only ones in the building.

My desk happened to be next to the copiers, and after a couple of hours of working, I heard what sounded like a stack of copy paper being thrown to the floor. But when I went to investigate, there was nothing out of place. I returned to find that the volume on my radio, which I had been listening to all morning, was turned way down. About ten minutes later, one of the other women left the building. The other woman came into my office a little later, asking if I had been walking past her office door. Apparently, someone had been passing by the open door to her office, but she had been unable to catch a good look. In addition to this, the phone system had been acting up all morning. Our intercom system runs through our phones and, for most of the morning, the small tone that precedes a page had been sounding throughout the building. A display on the phone, which tells the origin of the page, indicated that the pages were being made from the security office, which was locked up tight and empty for the weekend. Then the elevator, which only runs when called, began to travel randomly between floors. At this point, we decided to call it a day.

As I was waiting for the elevator, one more strange event happened. We were working on the top (sixth) floor at the time, and there is a locked stairway to the roof next to the elevator. Through the window on the door, I noticed that the lights in the roof stairwell were off. But when I turned back a moment later, they were on. The only switch for those lights is behind the locked stairwell door. By the time the elevator came, the lights were off again.

After that time, I personally experienced odd happenings here on several occasions. And I am not the only one to report these events. The most common occurrence that people report is the hearing of footsteps either directly behind them or just ahead. People have reported hearing what sounds like someone walking down the hallway, where there is clearly no one to be seen or when they know that the building is deserted. Others will have the feeling that someone is standing directly behind them, looking over their shoulder. But when they turn to look, there is no one there. Still others, especially those on the night staff, hear papers being shuffled, or the click of someone typing on a keyboard.

At first these events happened at off-hours, or at times when there were very few people in the building. But recently, in the months before I left the firm, things had begun happening during the normal workday. For example, a friend of mine was washing his hands in the restroom when he felt a hand come to rest on his shoulder.

He was notably startled, considering the wall-to-wall mirror he was standing in front of revealed that he was the only one in the bathroom.

An anonymous former employee included the account of her haunted ad agency in a letter to the author in the fall of 1999.

Rosehill Haunts

Author's photo.

One of the chapels at monumental Rosehill Cemetery is
allegedly attended by a loving—but long-gone—caretaker.

Another Batch of Phantoms from Ravenswood's Opulent Ossuary

IT'S NO NEWS THAT some of Chicago's most famous haunts are harbored by the sprawling Victorian enclosure named Rosehill Cemetery, an ossuary unmatched for history, art, and sheer size. Ghosthunters old and new have for many years made determined pilgrimages to this once-rural setting to scope out a number of sites, including the glass-enclosed monument to Frances Pearce and her infant daughter. Victims of tuberculosis who died just months apart, their passing was marked by a grieving husband and father with a breathtaking marble likeness of mother and daughter at rest together. On the anniversaries of their deaths, the pair are said to rise from the monument's pedestal, their figures enshrouded by a white mist that fills the encasement. A number of years ago, *The National Enquirer* featured a story on Rosehill's Hopkinson Mausoleum, a family tomb that became the center of a heated lawsuit when another prominent Chicago family made plans to build in front of the Hopkinson's sepulchre, a move that reportedly sparked a long-gone Charles Hopkinson to begin rattling chains inside his tomb. More chilling still are the reports of ghostly merchandiser Richard Warren Sears, who has been seen more than once wandering the dank halls of the cemetery's huge community mausoleum, presumably in search of his temporal arch-enemy, Aaron Montgomery Ward, buried just steps away from the Sears family room.

Beyond these folkloric phantasms, Rosehill hosts a much larger, varied, and believable gathering of ghost stories, from one end of its vast acreage to the other. Passers-by report the image of a young girl appearing at the Gothic window to the left and just below the bell tower at the Ravenswood gates. The girl is said to be Philomena Boyington, granddaughter of architect William W. Boyington, who built the Rosehill gateway in 1864. Little Philomena often played at the construction site while her grandpa worked. She died of pneumonia not long after the entry's completion.

Joining Miss Boyington in Rosehill's shadows is Elizabeth Archer, who committed suicide in aching response to the accidental death of her high school sweetheart, Arnold Fischel. Students at North Side Senn High School, their pairing was evidently approved by Archer's father, who erected to their memory the so-called Archer-Fischel Monument, where Elizabeth is sometimes spotted at chilly November dusks.

The teenaged Archer may find solace in the friendship of another set of lovers here who have been sighted between the commemorative Smith column in Section 11 and the Smith memorial bench near the intersection of sections 11 and 18. They appear distraught and, when approached about their well-being, calmly explain that they cannot leave, as they are buried nearby. At this, both vanish. Some believe that these unfortunate wanderers were star-crossed lovers who died as a result of their suicide pact: a drug overdose meant to keep them together despite their parents' disfavor. Whoever they are, a number of witnesses attest to their ongoing angst, including a Roman Catholic priest and a funeral director.

Freemasons and their fans will want to join ghosthunters at a rather lively memorial at Rosehill erected by the Lincoln Park Masonic Lodge, which had its charter revoked by the Grand Lodge of Joliet when the Lincoln Parkers were accused of dealings in the black arts. The defunct lodge's monument features a large sphere affixed to its pinnacle. Weighing in at several tons, the sphere has reportedly fallen off about once every ten years, affirming, some say, the divine disfavor of the underlying members.

Joining the banished brothers here is Gerhardt Foreman, a pal of Englishman Alistair Crowley, the so-called "wickedest man in the world," with whom Foreman studied for a number of years. Returning to the United States, Foreman founded the A.M.O.R.C., the Golden Dawn, and other Masonic orders, while dabbling in any number of esoteric pastimes. Buried here at Rosehill, Foreman's family mausoleum is said to have been chained shut to keep Gerhardt from wandering.

Keeping watch on Foreman and others is the phantom of Stephen Hansson, a turn-of-the-nineteenth-century caretaker and gravedigger who was murdered in his then-rural Lake View home and buried at Rosehill. Visitors infrequently catch a twilight glimpse of Hansson in his old coveralls, leaning on a spade in the driveway of the retaining vaults behind the May Chapel.

Darius Miller died too soon to be buried by Hansson, but no matter. Miller was buried in a replica of the Egyptian temple of Anubis, after dying as a result of the curse of King Tut. The curator of Egyptology at Chicago's Field Museum of Natural History at the time of the discovery of Tutankhamen's tomb, Miller was there when the ancient sepulchre was unsealed, and was thus among those marked for death by the famous curse. History reveals that all members of the archaeological team were dead within a year of the tomb's opening. Adding to Darius Miller's mysterious demise is the rumor of a blue light seen seeping from his tomb in the early morning hours of each May 1.

Such stories abound at Rosehill. Many visitors to the grave of Lulu Fellows are treated to the scent of fresh flowers as they leave coins, toys, and other tokens at Lulu's monument, an uncanny likeness encased in glass and labeled with the tragic epitaph: *Many Hopes Lie Buried Here.*

And legend has long held that visitors at the gravestone of Mary Shedden, allegedly poisoned by her own husband in 1931, will see one of two startling visions: a glimpse of Mary's warm, inviting face, or the leering skull of her hapless corpse. Skeptics brush off this tale, claiming that the stone's material (mica, a shimmering, gold-like substance) is responsible for these tricks of the eye.

Yet, those close to Rosehill's heart believe, just as they believe in the uncanny mobility of the Frank M. Baker monument, the statue of a graceful deer, that has been seen on many occasions far from its home over the Baker lot. In fact, while hurrying to his duties during an evening storm, former caretaker James Hutchenson caught a glimpse of this unmistakable animal "grazing" near the Ravenswood Avenue gates, only to find it back in place the next morning—lodged, as ever, in concrete.

The author is indebted to Michael McArthur, a Druid priest and Rogers Park resident, who alerted the author to Rosehill Cemetery's "other" haunts in his detailed, written tour of the site's supernatural legends.

CHICAGO AMERICAN HAUNTS

Reporter among the Spirits

ON THE NIGHT OF March 31, 1848, a deeply spiritual Pough-keepsie man named Andrew Jackson Davis sat straight up in bed, awakened by a voice which told him that the "work" had begun.

This cryptic "work" was to be realized as nothing less than the tedious but marvelous project of establishing communication with the dead. For it was on this same night that tiny Katherine Fox, a young girl whose family had long been disturbed by strange noises in their Hydesville, New York, home, had snapped her fingers at an invisible guest and commanded, *Here, old Splitfoot, do as I do!* When a responding "rap" came from the air, the Spiritualist movement was born.

Kate Fox's "spirit rapping" began the so-called modern communication with spirits through a structured technological system of Morse-like code. This type of spiritual telegraphing was only the first example of the trendiness of the nineteenth-century spirits, who used advances in technology, like automatic writing with graphite pencils, to prove their own existence. They also seemed to favor the fad of Mesmerism, a type of mental healing, whose patients sometimes claimed visitations with the dead, clairvoyance, and precognition when "magnetized." Andrew Jackson Davis had himself been a Mesmerist, familiar enough with that hypnotically induced step-off into the other sphere. Known locally as the "Poughkeepsie Seer" Davis claimed that, when hypnotized, he could communicate with those of other realms, who suggested to him ways for improving the human condition.

Confronted with the paradox of spiritualism in an age of mechanical positivism, historians long assumed the nineteenth-century Spiritualist movement to be just one more part of that era's revolt against rampant society—a physical and ideological neighbor of New York State's

Utopian communities. Remembered, when at all, as a quirk in the works of the century's larger-than-lifers (William Lloyd Garrison, Joshua Giddings, Harriet Beecher Stowe, Horace Greeley, William Cullen Bryant, James Fenimore Cooper, Elizabeth Cady Stanton, and others), the movement was much more to many others. In 1865, Theodore Parker observed that Spiritualism as a religion was more likely "to become the religion of America than in 156 A.D. that Christianity would be the religion of the Roman Empire." And although that prophecy in retrospect seems foolishly off the mark, the true principles of the phenomenon did become enmeshed in American thought and culture.

It was puzzlement rather than rapping spirits that haunted the movement's skeptics, like George Templeton Strong, disturbed by Spiritualism's popularity in "that enlightened nineteenth century." Still, although fraud would make the gullible easy prey for the movement, the promise of evidence of immortality inspired the rational minds of the age's most respected thinkers, and kept that "enlightened nineteenth century" utterly enchanted. In fact, it was the nineteenth-century fanaticism with empirical science that made Spiritualism seem so promising. Ironically materialistic, its increasing reliance on materialization of spirits prompted disgust in metaphysicians like Ralph Waldo Emerson. Few rallied around his opinion, however, as Emerson's peers abandoned transcendentalism, finding a kind of freedom in Spiritualism's removal of the ever-constricting "ifs." Spiritualists rejected supernaturalism, trumpeted the inviolability of natural law, demanded external facts rather than intuition, and threw their faith behind the progressive development of natural knowledge.

The weird marriage of the mechanical and the spiritual was an easy one for Americans, who in the years before Spiritualism's rage had marveled at inventions of innovators like Benjamin Franklin. As historian Werner Sollors recognized, Spiritualism was actually a sacralization of empiricism, an attempt to "find transcendental meaning in graphite pencils and gaslight, . . . batteries, locomotives, and the telegraph itself."

Ah, the telegraph! It was this single invention that opened wide the doors to Spiritualist possibility. For if real-time communication could be accomplished across thousands of miles of space, why not communication to other realms, where the dearly beloved reportedly reside. Benjamin Franklin, the telegraph's inventor, made frequent appearances at the séances of earlier times, thrilling mediums and sitters in his role of "heavenly inventor" of modern spirit communication.

With spiritual advocates like Franklin and earthbound proselytizers like Davis, and the support of a generous portion of the literary and philosophical giants of the age, Spiritualism won over a conservatively-estimated 1.5 million Americans who had rejected Orthodox Christianity in the belief that life had only so many questions, all of which humanity—innovative, rational, and clever—was quite capable of answering. Taking their regular places in séance parlors and Spiritualist churches, they sought evidence of the Unknown in the form of ectoplasmic hands and trivial information from the great beyond.

Though fraud and further development halted the thrust of the Spiritualist movement at the turn of the century, many Spiritualist churches and camps remained, the latter as havens where mediums and believers might come together to live in community with the other-worldlies who were summoned nightly at camp séances. The most famous of these camps is still in existence today. Lily Dale, considered the home of the Spiritualist movement, is situated in north central Chautauqua County, southwest of Buffalo, New York. In its heyday, the population of Lily Dale swelled each summer from 300 to 2,000: the 1,700 "vacationers" were Spiritualists from all over the world, drawn to Lily Dale as students of "survivalism," the existence of life after death. Lily Dale was so prominent in the Spiritualist culture that the original Fox home was relocated there. This was the very place where a murdered peddler had manifested himself to the Fox family and communicated with Kate Fox on that fateful night in 1848.

Camps like Lily Dale reaped huge benefits from the international wars of the twentieth century. Just as the American Civil War had sent countless mourners to séance parlors hoping for contact with lost husbands and sons, so did the bereaved of the World Wars seek comfort in the medium's alleged abilities. So it was that Lily Dale was at the peak of its popularity in 1942, when Ann Marsters, a reporter for the old *Chicago American*, was sent there to do a series of articles on the puzzling Spiritualist hub. Sitting through a number of séances, the communications from Marsters's dead relatives fell short of her critical ear. Before her departure from Lily Dale, however, an incident occurred that threw the hard-boiled journalist's sensibilities decidedly out of whack. During one sitting, Marsters was introduced to her "spirit guide," a sort of personal escort to the spirit world. "Red Rose," the quirky spirit assigned to the no-nonsense Marsters, shocked the reporter by revealing to the other sitters that Marsters had fixed a tear in her coat lining with a safety pin before leaving her hotel that evening, an assertion that, remarkably, was true.

Back in Chicago, Marsters typed up a batch of articles in her home office, chronicling her experiences at the mysterious camp. Ever rational, she kept her run-in with "Red Rose" out of the text. On a Friday afternoon, a copy boy came to pick up the manuscript of Marsters's first article, along with a carbon copy. Anxious about the safe delivery of the piece, Marsters reminded the messenger to hand-deliver the article to the Sunday editor, as the first of the write-ups was to appear that coming Sunday. The boy assured her he would.

On Saturday afternoon, however, a frantic call came from Marsters's editor, demanding the copy for the first article. The panic-stricken Marsters informed him that she had finished the article on Friday and had given it to the copy boy to deliver. Questioning the messenger, both editor and reporter were baffled, and enraged, when the boy could not remember what he had done with the article.

Hopeless of ever re-writing the piece in time for the deadline, Marsters rushed down to the *Chicago American* offices, determined to find the missing article herself. Despairing of her task after an hour of searching, she suddenly remembered Red Rose. Desperate, and with an almost religious fervor, Marsters closed her eyes and called on her spirit guide for rescue: *You found the safety pin in my coat. Please, Red Rose, please find my article . . .*

Then, as if walking in her sleep, Marsters strode over to the pay phone on the other side of the newsroom and opened a tattered directory.

Inside, complete and perfect, lay Marsters's article, ready for the presses, courtesy of the Other Side.

The nearly forgotten story of Red Rose and Ann Marsters was saved for posterity by Beth Scott and Michael Norman in their popular volume Haunted Heartland. *Background on the Spiritualist movement, its origins and nature, were provided by* In Search of White Crows: Spiritualism, Parapsychology and American Culture; The Heyday of Spiritualism; *and the following articles: Robert W. Delp, "A Spiritualist in Connecticut: Andrew Jackson Davis, the Hartford years, 1850-1854," New England Quarterly. Vol. 53 (September, 1980); Laurence R. Moore, "Spiritualism and science:*

reflections on the first decade of the spirit rappings." American Quarterly. *Vol. 24 (October, 1972); Werner Sollors, "Dr. Benjamin Franklin's celestial telegraph, or Indian blessings to gas-lit American drawing-rooms,"* American Quarterly. *Vol. 35 (Winter, 1983).*

BUCKTOWN PUB HAUNTS

Photo by D. Cowan.

Some say that the popular Bucktown Pub is still managed by its past owner.

Another Round of Wrath

IN A TOWN WHERE Prohibition never quite caught on, imbibing ghosts have been ever on tap, hitting the ethereal bottle while haunting flesh-and-blood patrons. Witness the famed Red Lion pub on north Lincoln Avenue, where a dark-haired phantom named Sharon appears to bartenders and barflies alike, screams bloody murder from the locked women's bathroom, and generally carouses with a host of fellow haunts, including a swaggering cowboy and a mustachioed Slovak.

Recall Frank Giff of north Broadway's Edinburgh Castle Pub (now the Old St. Andrew's Inn) who, in the 1960s, drank himself to death in his favorite booth, where he remains today, running his ghostly fingers down the legs of red-headed female customers.

These spots have been known as Chicago's haunted taverns for decades, but they are not alone in their harboring of invisibles. In fact, in and out of the city, barroom ghosts are as numerous and diverse as the gin mills that sprang up here after the passage of the Volstead Act—and as boisterous.

When Bucktown was still Bucktown, before the outsiders came, locals delighted when a new pub opened up at 1658 W. Cortland Street, on the site of a favorite old tavern. To the chagrin of neighborhood regulars, the barroom had been closed for two years after its former owner, a man remembered only as Wally, shot himself in the upstairs apartment sometime in the late 1970s. With Wally's widow still in residence, a new owner eventually reopened the establishment, under the impression that she finally had a place of her own. Not six months after the opening, however, she had become convinced that Wally was still very much in charge.

By the mid-1990s, the owner and patrons were regularly reporting peculiar events, notably the mysterious movement of increasingly heavy objects, from stacks of cardboard coasters to beer bottles, first empty, then full, to a jumbo-sized trophy. When a Rolling Rock sign fell on top of one of the bartenders, the employee quit. What would be next?

Unlike the Red Lion's delightful Sharon and the playful Giff at Old St. Andrew's, Wally was downright nasty. Patrons who remember him recall a grouchy, verbally abusive tyrant, who would perch on one of his own barstools, ordering around both the bartenders and the customers. His wrath was arbitrary in life and after. The ghost, it seemed, would roam the place at will, picking on whomever offended his indiscernible tastes, sometimes throwing objects at the offensive patron or employee to underscore his opinion.

The new owner took Wally's moodiness in stride, usually. Occasionally, she would lose her temper with the temperamental phantom and chew out the air in a fit of exasperation, an act that probably won her a fair measure of the wraith's respect.

These days, Bucktown has come a long way from the days when Wally held court at his beloved watering hole on west Cortland Street. Most say the neighborhood has progressed significantly, brilliantly, its newcomers congratulating themselves for "saving" another neighborhood from becoming a slum. Bask as they might in their own wonderfulness, let them steer clear of the Bucktown Pub. There, the opinionated Wally waits, guarding the late, great Bucktown and his own favorite haunt, ready to knock over the next one through the door.

An account of the strange goings-on at the Bucktown Pub was presented in "Haunting Bar Reviews," **Barfly,** *October/November 1994.*

WATER TOWER HAUNTS

Author's photo.

This symbol of the city shelters a grim reminder of the town's biggest night.

A Haunting Memento of the City's Hallmark Disaster

AFTER THE GREAT FIRE of 1871, when the smoke had cleared and the ashes settled, the sun rose on Chicago's desolation and then shone on it. In his "Five Months After" essay which appeared in the *Chicago Times* in April, 1872, editor Everett Chamberlain reiterated an American joke which had been enjoyed in recent months, especially by Chicagoans: "the joke wherein a citizen of some far-off town was represented as rushing with mad haste to the railway station . . . because, as he said, he must reach Chicago . . . or they would have the whole town built up again before he could get a view of the ruins." And it was true.

The swift, phoenix-like emergence of the post-fire city—stronger, bigger, better than before—gained Chicago a permanent and worldwide reputation as an unstoppable metropolis: "The City that Works." Yet, while Chicagoans quickly dismissed the disaster in favor of the future, the first few days found Chicagoans filled with despair and the nation and world desperate for details.

Full of the monstrous news and eager for sympathetic ears, stunned Chicagoans wrote to friends and relations around the world, sending much-anticipated news of the state of the city. Without photos or newsreels to provide a vision of the disaster, out-of-towners relied on the vivid descriptions of the fire's own witnesses. Chicagoans' letters regarding the disaster remain one of the city's most precious historical resources, providing as they do keen and colorful witness to the great conflagration. Many of these letters' authors document their own destruction, tracing in a rush of words their overnight falls from wealth and luxury to impoverished homelessness. Others, luckier, report on the misfortune of others.

Anna Higginson, wife of George M. Higginson, real estate broker, lived with her husband on Dearborn Street, just north of Chicago Avenue. While the city still smoldered, she sent word of the fire to her friend, Mrs. Mark Skinner, in Europe with her husband at the time, including literary pictures of the fire's attendant madness:

> Mrs. Winston saved a pink silk dress trimmed with lace, but very little else; one lady had a carriage full of party dresses & another a half dozen bonnets. One man was seen running from the fire with two immense turnips & another with a piece of broken furniture . . . .

But while these snapshots peppered the city's memory in the days after the fire, most of the lasting remembrance was vivid film, destined to replay itself forever in the city's mind:

> . . . [T]he fire worked up gradually along the North Branch & the instant the wind caught it the fire was hurled the whole length of the city; in that way our house was burned at last.
>
> As I went out of it & saw the vine-covered walls & the windows filled with flowers all shining so peacefully in the moonlight, it seemed impossible to realize that in a few moments the smoke & flame I saw all around me would seize that too & that I was look-ing upon my home for the last time.

This destitution would be, for most, a temporary condition, yet an unquestionable blanket of loss was fixed forever:

> We . . . rode to the West Side in company with thousands of other refugees like ourselves—dusty, smoky, forlorn in every way . . . the air full of blinding dust & smoke & behind us our ruined homes, with all their years of accumulated treasures & associa-tions of every kind. It is for those I grieve . . . my Mother's Bible, the clothing & toys of my dead children. . . .

Incredibly but typically, the unspeakable destruction left behind by the "memorable conflagration" written of by *Chicago Times* editor Everett Chamberlain five months after the fire was not exclusively attributable to the fire itself. In fact, a significant portion of the damage was the work of looters and thieves, who took advantage of the chaos and the preoccupation of police forces to plunder the burning city. "The like of this sight since Sodom & Gomorra has never met human vision," wrote Jonas Hutchinson, lawyer and notary. "No pen can tell what a ruin this is." But he tried. To his mother in New Hampshire, Hutchinson penned his own testimony of the fire and the blackness that described far more than its charred ruins:

> . . . [T]he city is thronged with desperadoes who are plunder-ing & trying to set new fires. The police are vigilant. Thousands of special police are on duty. Every block has its patrolmen and instructions are explicit to each officer to shoot any man who acts suspicious and will not answer when spoken [to] the second time. Several were shot & others hung to lamp posts last night under these instructions.
>
> . . . The roughs are improving the time to sack & pillage. The city is in darkness.

The neighborhood hit hardest shows little sign of the madness that once prevailed here. Fixed at its heart, the old water works are like quaint garden ornaments in this happy corner at Chicago and Michigan Avenues, the Water Tower itself converted to a cheerful visitors center. Poverty, too, is just a word here, its reality unfathomable in the shopping frenzy of Michigan Avenue's Disneyland atmosphere. Least evident is the lawlessness of autumn, 1871, when looters swung from the lamp-posts, desperately subdued by attempts at law and order during a reign of absolute terror.

Yet, just as the Water Tower itself forces the fire's memory on all who pass its castellated remains, so too do some of the players in that drama. In an upper window of the old tower, before its renovation and even now, passers-by have occasionally seen the figure of a man, limp and pallid, dangling by a rope around his neck. Workers in the infor-mation center profess ignorance of the sightings, testifying that memory alone haunts this structure. Those eager to search the digs of the reported wraith are out of luck, too. The actual tower is closed to the public.

Today, many historians claim that the execution of the Great Fire's looters is a myth. Accidental deaths did occur, of course, in the course of law enforcement. But the wide-scale and officially-approved hanging of criminals is the stuff of legend. Still, the letters remain, their authors' descriptions of the hangings as vivid now as ever. And even those who disregard them may someday catch a glimpse of the proof they need: one hapless witness to the rule that crime doesn't pay, paying his own dues forever in the city's signature tower.

Victims' accounts of the Great Fire were extracted from letters published in The Great Chicago Fire *(CHS).*

UPPER PENINSULA HAUNTS

Author's photo.

The woods across southwest suburban Maple Lake, where Chicagoans
have long gathered to view a local manifestation of "ghost lights."

Light-Hearted Mysteries

THE LUMINOUS PHENOMENA KNOWN as ghost lights or spook lights have been sighted in many parts of the world for countless generations. Making their homes in rural areas of a diversity of nations, including Japan, England, and the United States, these lights, usually balls of white or yellow iridescence, draw hundreds, or in some places, thousands, of sightseers each year, all hoping for (and typically rewarded with) a glimpse of these peculiar entities.

Ghost lights are often surprisingly reliable. Unlike other spontaneous phenomena studied by *psi* researchers, such as hauntings and poltergeists, they tend to appear at a certain time each evening, for a regular period of time, during set times of the year. As such, ghost lights have attracted determined investigators, including the local Ghost Research Society, based in southwest suburban Oak Lawn, which has counted ghost light investigation among its top priorities. The society has identified a number of characteristics shared by all of these lights, from the most notorious ones, including those viewed at Marfa, Texas, since at least 1883, to the light sighted in recent years off the 95th Street Overlook at southwest suburban Maple Lake: a glowing ball said to hover about fifty feet above the ground. Common denominators include the rural setting of these lights, their resistance to attempts to fix their points of origin, their tendency to react to noise and light, and their association with local tragic folklore, most frequently the old tale of the headless ghost searching for his noggin with the aid of an ethereal lamp.

Chicagoans encountering the Maple Lake Light will want to seek out another fairly local light, which may be sought during vacation days in neighboring Michigan. Known interchangeably as the Paulding Light and the Watersmeet Light for the towns between which the light appears, the almost nightly phenomenon has been mystifying locals and tourists for at least 34 years. In fact, a number of residents of this Upper Peninsula region claim to have been seeing the light for generations, but the first reported sighting occurred in the mid-1960s, when a group of teenagers decided to park one night along a boggy stretch of the old Military Road known as Dog Meadow.

Echoing modern-day reports of UFOs, the driver's testimony held that a brilliant light had filled their car. Searching for the source of the illumination, the group noticed a light which seemed suspended over the power line running along the road to Paulding. Terrified, the group fled the site, heading straight to the sheriff to report what they had seen.

The experience touched off a sensation. Ever since, carloads of curiosity seekers have been keeping vigil along that old stretch of Highway 45, halfway between Paulding and Watersmeet, hoping to spot the mystifying light. On almost any clear night of the year, the northwest horizon will yield a vision of the weather-balloon-sized light, its intensity varying at regular intervals, from several seconds to nearly ten minutes. Some motorists have sworn that their engines stalled or died as the light moved above their cars. Skeptics say, *No way*, identifying the illumination as car lights rounding the pinnacle of Cemetery Hill, five miles away.

Such skeptics do not count scientists among them, the latter of whom tie ghost lights to seismologic events. These theorists say that the pressure of glacial ice compressed the earth's crust and that ghost lights are the luminous gases released as the earth gradually expands to its original state. Other scientists have linked unexplained lights to the occurrence of earthquakes and regularly track ghost lights in an attempt to locate natural warning signs of an approaching catastrophe.

Romantic locals, though aware of the legitimate possibilities, choose to offer tourists a more compelling explanation for the Paulding-Watersmeet Light. One folktale ties the light to the tragic death of a mail carrier and his team of sled dogs, killed at Dog Meadow more than a century ago. Another, this one in step with classic ghost light legends, tells of a murdered railway engineer wandering the old railroad grade near the light's sighting point.

To reach the vantage point for the Paulding-Watersmeet Light, set out at dusk from Watersmeet, Michigan, traveling north on Highway 45 for about four miles. Take Robbins Pond Road to the top of the second hill. Once there, simply park and wait. Disappointment is unlikely.

Information on the Paulding-Watersmeet Light was provided by North Shore resident R. Irwin, who witnessed the light during a trip to the region in the mid-1990s. Additional general information on ghost or spook lights was provided by Mary Ellen Guiley's Encyclopedia of Ghosts and Spirits, *which includes the Ghost Research Society's findings on the characteristics of such lights.*

MUSIC BOX HAUNTS

Author's photo.

On revitalized Southport Avenue, the old
Music Box Theatre still lights up the night.

Legend of a Silver Screen

THOSE UNFAMILIAR WITH THE whys and wherefores of hauntings often assume that a spirit lingers only when there remains a debt to be paid, vengeance to be had, or a message to be given a left-behind loved one. Not so. In fact, some of the most notable apparitions are those that remain simply because they love their work too much to trade it in, even for paradise. These are the untiring laborers in love, those individuals closely and loyally tied to a particular institution: the founder of a school, the head of a library's board of directors, or the longtime pastor of a close-knit parish. Dedicated in life to the care of their special niche, in death, too, these figures aim to keep an eye on their lifelong passions. On Southport Avenue, in Chicago's Lakeview neighborhood, the Music Box Theatre remains the hotly-guarded haven of the film house's original and lasting manager—a quirky neighborhood man known only as Whitey.

For nearly half a century, Whitey and his wife devoted endless hours to the theater, from the summer night in 1929 when the Music Box screened its first film, *Mother's Boy*, starring Morton Downey, through the second- and third-run movie days of the 1930s, '40s, and '50s, right up to its final days of regular operation in the mid-1970s, after which the theater was leased by a string of half-legitimate operators, who screened everything from Arabic feature films to pornography.

From the beginning, Whitey was a beloved fixture of old Lakeview, maintaining in particular a satisfying balance of love and hate between himself and the neighborhood kids, the latter of whom might be treated to free candy one night only to have their photos pasted up in the lobby's "rogues gallery" the next, having crossed Whitey's delicate temper in some vague way.

On the night before Thanksgiving, November 24, 1977, Whitey walked the same two blocks he'd walked for nearly 50 years to close the Music Box for the evening. Remaining longer than necessary in the place he loved best, he fell asleep on the lobby couch—forever.

After his death, the theater was closed. It would be six long years before the Music Box would again open for regular business. When it did, in 1983, it opened with a passion.

An exhaustive, four-month restoration preceded the screening of *Wabash Avenue* and *In Old Chicago*, two Hollywood revivals slated to pay tribute to the city that lived 54 years earlier when the Music Box had first opened its doors. With the return of the reels, and the spit and polish of caring owners, came the theater's old friend, Whitey, reporting for work as ever.

Since the reopening, employees have credited Whitey with finding lost items and solving problems with business. He is even supposed to have critiqued an unsatisfactory organist by dropping both organ draperies while the poor musician tried to play. An effective, if invisible, overseer, the staff of the theater considers Whitey their "Manager Emeritus."

The story of Whitey, the Music Box's beloved curmudgeon, was related to the author by several of the neighborhood's longtime residents. Information on the Music Box Theatre was provided by the theater's wonderful Web site: www.musicboxtheatre.com. *The site includes a brief outline of the theatre's history and haunting and suggests some further reading for the theater's fans, including fine pieces in* Theatre Classics *(December 1992, p. 20) and* Chicago *magazine (September 1991, p. 73), which were also consulted for the telling of this tale.*

CAMP FORT DEARBORN HAUNTS

Photo by D. Cowan.

Coming upon the clearing at Camp Fort Dearborn, once
a popular site for Chicago Boy Scouts' overnighters.

Ill-Prepared

THE WORLD OVER, CAMPFIRES have long gone hand in hand with ghost stories, and Chicago is no exception. For generations, Boy and Girl Scouts, Explorer Scouts, and tent-dwellers of all ages have thrilled to stories passed on through many summers and many eager ears. To be sure, "round-the-fire tales" are some of storytellers' most chilling, based as they are on the fables known today as urban legends. These are the maniac tales, the man-eating-monster tales, the axe-wielding-murderer tales. Silly as they seem in daylight, they are stories that speak volumes to our primitive and urban fears of the dark, of the sometimes-alien natural world, and of the woods in particular.

Chicago is no stranger to this ancient fear of the forest. But Chicagoans' fear of their urban preserves, gathered under the care of the Forest Preserve District of Cook County, is supported not only by tall tales, but by very real dangers. Unquestionable and plentiful oddities live here in the form of would-be rapists and muggers, love addicts searching for impromptu partners, and an army of amateur occultists. All add to the dark lure of these expanses, mixing with local folklore, ongoing rumors, and frequent brushes of visitors with the unseen, and creating a chaos of indecipherable intrigue that leers from between the trees.

One of the most common of the many unusual phenomena reported by forest preserve visitors is the sound of chanting or breathing. Hikers in the Northwest Side LaBagh Woods, the southwest suburban Rubio Woods, and other woods claim that their walks have turned suddenly to nightmares when these waves of sound arise all around them. Though the unsettling incidents occur when the woods are empty of other visitors, some claim that these sounds can be tied to real beings; namely, the Satan worshippers that have been vandalizing the forest preserves since at least the 1960s. Self-schooled in the ways of nature, they say, these neo-occultists steal into the woods, intent on scaring the dickens out of anyone out for innocent fun. Power-hungry and exceedingly territorial, they are supposed to delight in clearing "their" woods of the uninitiated.

Others, less skeptical and well aware of the documented presence of these vandals, believe that it is the rituals they practice, and not the practitioners themselves, that take the credit for the haunting of the city's preserves. These woods were healthy, beautiful sites, they say, until the amateur evil-doers conjured up the forests' spirits without knowing how to send them back when they were finished with them. Now, all Hell is on the loose within these confines: no place, to be sure, for a picnic.

Though the Forest Preserve District has little to offer in the way of official campsites, there are a few spots that have been used for this purpose by the Chicago Area Boy Scouts of America, one of them the now-abandoned Camp Fort Dearborn, situated just north of O'Hare Airport between Chicago and suburban Park Ridge.

Abandoned. No one will say why the B.S.A. left this conveniently local getaway to the birds, but some old Scouts have memories of the last of those Fort Dearborn nights:

It was during my time with Troop 3865 during the 1970s. Most of our overnighters were held some distance from Chicago, with other troops from the area or even the entire state; occasionally, however, our troop would have overnighters at a more local site, and this was what brought us at times to Camp Fort Dearborn; we would have an annual ceremony in the forest there to welcome new members to our troop. There would be a large fire built in a clearing for the event, which was centered around a brick and timber podium that had been built by earlier members for such ceremonies, along with awards presentations and other functions.

During one of these annual campouts at Fort Dearborn we had planned the welcoming ceremony for around ten o'clock in the evening. We scouts would camp in the large field past the preserve entrance and, to get to the ceremonial site, we would have to hike a short distance through the woods to the clearing. This particular night, just before the commencement time, we set out as usual for the site, obviously alone along the trail. When we reached the clearing, we got the bonfire started and, when it was going strong, took our places around it. As the new troop members filed in to the clearing from the trail, the ceremony began.

All was well and usual for the first half-hour or so. Then, at around 10:30 P.M., the group of us—numbering about thirty—began to hear a rustling in the woods all around us, as if the trees were being stirred frantically by someone—but on all sides. After several minutes of this commotion, another sound began: that of a distinct and heavy breathing, as if dozens of people were breathing in and out very loudly and in sync with each other.

None of us knew what to do. Calling out and searching the trees with flashlights revealed no one, though the sounds kept on. The ceremony was concluded early, and we were led quickly back to our camp, approximately three-fourths of a mile away.

The next morning, we returned to the clearing to clean up after the hasty retreat we had made the night before and found the ceremonial podium vandalized with Satanic-type carvings— "666," "LSD," and "Devil Dog"—along with other markings. Several nooses had been hung in the trees surrounding the clearing, and small fires had been lit around its circumference.

Though there had been no sign of anyone else in the surrounding woods, it was obvious that others had been close. Still, there was no way, in our minds, of connecting the presumably small gathering of people that must have followed us the night before with the incredible sound we'd heard during our ceremony—that sound of the steady, unified, and deliberate breathing of, as I said, literally dozens of people, absolutely upon us, that we couldn't even see.

The chilling story of Camp Fort Dearborn, only one of many such tales from the Forest Preserve District of Cook County, was related to the author by an anonymous witness in a written account during the summer of 2000.

CHANNING ELEMENTARY HAUNTS

THE OLD CEMETERY 1843-1945

THEIR WORLDLY TASKS COMPLETED
ELGIN'S PIONEERS WERE LAID TO REST
IN THIS HALLOWED GROUND

ELGIN AREA HISTORICAL SOCIETY--1966

Photo by D. Cowan.

A stone marker at Channing School commemorates those once
buried here, when the land comprised Elgin's first cemetery.

Scared Smart in Elgin

It SHOULD NOT SURPRISE that the old and storied northern Illinois town of Elgin should have more than its share of invisible citizens. Generations ago, Al Capone's rum-runners considered Elgin practically an annex of Chicago proper, as its residents added a lot to the treasury of the Mob. Elgin is suitably stuffed full of rambling farmhouses said to harbor shades of gangsters, hookers, and those who crossed them; and the roads in and out of town are packed with phantom Fords, sliding in and out of vision at night.

But Capone's Mob isn't the only presence here. Elgin plays host to a wide variety of lingering, lost souls, good and bad. Consider the Schreiners, whose Jefferson Avenue house has a bathroom full of playful, but invisible, children, who make merry in the weeks between Thanksgiving and Christmas. Witness the living room of Albert Cox and Reggie Stephens that developed an icy air when they decided to change the paint color. Wisely restoring the original color, the temperature rose again. The Minetti family shared its Hill Avenue house with a group of strangers who would visit their rooms at night with footsteps loud enough to wake the owners. And diners at a downtown eatery called Marina's have long witnessed the antics of "Marian the Librarian"—a former worker from the building's old library who toys with the light switches and throws the dishes around.

Plentiful as they are, Elgin's living residents find their ghostly citizens pretty lovable, interpreting their presence as another sign of the historical richness of which Elginites are so proud—with one exception.

In the 1940s, the hill that held Elgin's first cemetery was razed to prepare the site for an athletic field. By then, all of the bodies were relocated to other sites. Unsettling it was then, when, in the 1960s, the basement of the future Channing Elementary School was dug, and a multitude of assorted bones came up with the clay. Horrified school officials called for the removal of the now-unidentifiable remains.

According to the story, construction workers weren't quite as unnerved. In 1990, Principal Clark White told the *Sun-Times* that workers treated the dead with total disrespect, putting bones in their colleagues' cars and lunch boxes.

One known grave remains in the school's vicinity: that of William Hackman, whose occupant rests in a corner of the adjacent Channing Park. Students at the school have claimed that the gravestone of Hackman is difficult to read. Even on still days, they say, leaves swirl around the stone, preventing visitors from deciphering the name. Other children have reported seeing blue people rising out of the ground around the stone, which is said to vibrate from an unseen force.

Though children's tales were dismissed in the school's early years, the 1990s ushered in a new era of belief, when teachers, parents and staff members began reporting their own run-ins with something unseen: an elevator that freely moved from floor to floor without being summoned, a hydraulic door that opened and closed by itself, its slam reverberating throughout the building, and invisible trespassers running on the roof.

The Channing phenomena included countless reports of ghostly name-calling and laughter, the latter so bone-chilling that a former janitor locked himself in the principal's office and called the boss's home number in tears. Other night workers began reporting dark figures strolling the hallways, and teachers marveled at the sound of scratching in the walls, as if someone were trying to claw his way out. Though spokespersons for the school viewed the noises as explainable, there was no stopping them or the chills they sent down many a Channing spine.

More than 30 years after the building of Channing Elementary School, the reports keep coming. Though they are plentiful, the explanations anticipated by administrators have not been forthcoming. Adults do what they do best in such cases: they ignore the nature of the phenomena, accepting the experiences as authentic but dismissing them as "natural." And the children? Well, whenever possible, they put ample distance between themselves and Channing School, afraid of what they might see in an upstairs window, afraid of hearing their name spoken by an unseen summoner.

At night, they just stay away.

Historian Mike Alft furnished the author with a number of newspaper articles regarding Elgin's phantoms, including "House-ghosts: Elgin homeowners have chilling tales to tell about some spirited—and spooky— visitors" (Chicago Tribune, *October 30, 1992);* "'Marian the librarian' is Facaccia's friendly ghost" (Elgin Daily Courier-News, *October 29, 1997);* "Haunted home holds no horror" (Elgin Daily Courier-News, *October 30, 1987); and "Spooky doings raise Elgin school's spirits"* (Sun-Times, *October 30, 1990), the latter of which covered the haunting of Channing Elementary School.*

FIELD MUSEUM HAUNTS

Author's photo.

Secret sharers love the enigmatic Field Museum,
an intriguing cache of ancient exotica.

Unclassified Specimens

ORIGINALLY **FOUNDED AS THE** Columbian Museum of Chicago, the city's Field Museum of Natural History was born in conjunction with the World's Fair of 1893, the Columbian Exposition, where the city displayed massive collections researchers had gathered into anthropological and biological displays. In the early 1920s, the museum moved its collections from its exposition site in Jackson Park to its current home on the lakefront, where it fixes one point in the triangle of institutions comprising Chicago's popular and relatively new "museum campus": the Field, the Adler, and the Shedd, all connected by landscaped pedestrian pathways. With more than 20 million specimens crammed into its many halls and storerooms, the Field has retained, many times magnified, its original power to thrill the audiences that stream through the museum's exhibits season upon season.

Part of the mystique of the Field can be explained by the cultural diversity of its collections, artifacts dripping with ancient intrigue and reeking of esoterica. Another part can be traced to the army of staff members that toil behind the scenes and around the clock in its countless labs and workrooms. Here, biologists, anthropologists, geologists, and zoologists carry out their research, registering anywhere from uneventful to earth-shattering.

This double-edged intrigue has led to the telling of many tales about Chicago's Field Museum. When, in 1996, the film *The Ghost and the Darkness* was released, chronicling the history of the so-called "Maneaters of Tsavo," a pair of African lions who killed more than 130 railroad workers in the late nineteenth century, longtime rumors resurfaced regarding the lions' carcasses, which have been part of the Field's collections since the mid-1920s, when they were sold to the museum by Lieutenant Colonel John Henry Patterson, who shot the lions in 1898. Patterson, chief engineer of the British government's project to build a railway bridge over East Africa's Tsavo River, wrung his hands for nine long months as scores of his men fell prey to the lions, who are guessed to have resorted to man-eating out of sheer hunger when an outbreak of disease killed off much of their natural prey.

The Lions of Tsavo, now highlighted with a detailed exhibit at the Field, are worthy of the story attributed to their name. Though their taxidermied appearance comes up shy of the lions' original statures (one measured more than nine and a half feet at the time of death), their dreadful natures still seem nearly tangible. It is not surprising that the legend of the animals, enhanced by the mystique of their African origin and dramatically underscored by their imposing physical presence, has given rise to new stories of strange behavior: peripheral glimpses of movement in the lions' display case, shifting of the animals' positions between viewings, their occasional disappearance altogether, and terrifying noises emanating from the exhibit hall.

Another of the museum's permanent exhibits, *Inside Ancient Egypt,* has also played host to a number of paranormal reports, namely of the sound of screams coming from the rooms housing the mummy displays that, some claim, inspired the recent film *The Relic,* an ancient-horror movie set in Chicago's natural history museum. One mummy in particular, an ancient fellow named Hawrar, occasionally catapults his own sarcophagus off the display stand and onto the floor, several feet away. Security guards discover the movement when they investigate a loud, gunshot-like sound that precedes the phenomenon. Though many believe that Hawrar takes midnight strolls through the museum on the nights when his casket goes haywire, few have seen the man behind the mummy. Yet, the museum admits to the odd activity, and employees like Pamela Buczkowske, a circulation clerk at the museum, have their own twilight run-ins with a decidedly Egyptian manifestation in the building's darkening hallways:

> I had been at the Field Museum for about two years. One evening after closing I was headed back to my office. I had taken the east center staircase down to the ground level. Off to my left was a short hallway I used to get back to where I worked. The hall is all but gone now. A new elevator was installed there, and the Egypt store was housed in that area.

As I walked down the stairs, I was surprised to see what I thought was a visitor coming toward me. Normal closing time was five o'clock; we had been closed for twenty minutes already. What didn't dawn on me until later was the fact that I could not see the upper body of the person. A shadow covered it at any angle.

I hurried up to the person to tell them that the museum was closed and he or she (I couldn't tell if it was a man or woman) would have to leave. But suddenly, the figure turned into the Egypt exhibit. I was practically on the person's heels, yet when I entered the exhibit, there was no one there. There wasn't even the sound of footfalls. I walked around the dark exhibit for a few minutes and found nothing.

Now, there are three ways to get out of the exhibit, and one gets locked at 4:45, on the first floor. The other two are on the ground floor, and I checked them out. One was locked, and the other would have brought the person right to me.

At first, I didn't really think I saw a ghost, and I wasn't scared. I did a little bit of investigating and found out a few things that I didn't realize at that time. One was the lighting. It wasn't dark enough to cover any part of the person I saw. Two was that the person never even acknowledged my presence. He or she had to have seen me coming toward them. The third thing occurred to me when a guard and I re-enacted what I saw. The lighting was the same and, as I'd suspected, there was no shadow over the upper part of his body.

I could see him perfectly.

Field Museum literature furnished background information on the strange goings-on at Inside Ancient Egypt *and on the story of the Man-Eaters of Tsavo. Anonymous sources told the tales of the latter exhibit's apparent haunting. Readers may exhaust themselves reading fascinating accounts of both exhibits by purchasing any of the many related books available in the museum shop. Pamela Buckowske furnished the author with a written account of her own Field Museum encounter, which she related in the winter of 1999, one of a number of such tales reported to the author by various persons.*

FORD CENTER HAUNTS

Photo by Bruce Nicholson.

This Montrose Cemetery monument to the victims of the
Iroquois Theatre Fire has hosted eerie phenomena since its erection.

A Fiendish Inferno Takes the "Absolutely Fireproof" Iroquois

CHICAGO IS A DEAR friend to disaster. From the 1812 massacre on the Lake Michigan dunes to the 1915 capsizing of the *Eastland* steamer on the Chicago River, to the crash of Flight 191 in the spring of 1979, the city has exchanged lives for infamy time and time again, establishing Chicago as an unlucky town. In particular, fire has battled the town's heart an astonishing number of times, marking the passage of decades with blazing reminders of the fallibility of our grandest plans. From pre-founding infernos that reduced whole blocks to cinders, to the infamous fire of 1871, to the unthinkable fire that, in 1958, ended the lives of more than 90 children at Our Lady of the Angels School, fire has been to Chicago an enemy, always waiting around the next corner, eager for heartache and headlines.

Despite the reaping of lives, many of them young, and the destruction of incalculable property, fire has not only destroyed but created. Perhaps the most famous example of this idea is the plan of Chicago itself, the way to which was opened by the wholesale destruction of the city by the Great Fire. In fact, a number of years ago, the City of Chicago formally thanked Catherine O'Leary for keeping the cow that started it all. It was because of that fire, they said, that Chicago, with its grid system and great vistas, is as beautiful and sensible as it is today. More soberly, the Our Lady of the Angels fire inspired fast and sweeping changes in fire safety codes around the country, as did another, early Chicago inferno: the devastating 1903 fire at the old Iroquois Theatre.

December 30, 1903 found thousands of Chicago children in the throes of leisure. Christmas had come and gone, but this was only Wednesday, and five days remained before the start of school. Ahead lay the New Year's festivities and, for many, days on the town with siblings, cousins, and friends, the groups of cheerful youngsters snaking through the Loop, headed up by weary mothers and aunts.

Turn-of-the-century Chicago was nothing to sniff at; the sights and sounds of its bustling downtown district were enough to hold the most insatiable adolescent in awe of its sheer variety. The usual fare consisted of enormous department store windows, packed with untold goods, street vendors hawking their own wares, a never-ending throng of people clad in all manner of dress and rushing to a thousand appointments, a crush of horses and wagons, and above it all, the thundering elevated train, carrying carloads of passengers over the crush of life below.

But today was even better.

For a Christmas holiday treat, nearly 2,000 schoolchildren and their chaperones were due at a special matinee performance of *Mr. Blue Beard*, starring popular comedian Eddie Foy. The venue was the new Iroquois Theatre, a peach of a theatre that had opened only five weeks earlier on Randolph Street. Built like a rock with the latest in safety equipment, the palace-like lobby elicited many an ooh and aah from the people who piled in that December afternoon. They would be the last accolades that the Iroquois would hear.

The first act of the upbeat musical passed without incident, the audience delighting at the antics of the cast, the luxury of the surroundings, and the impressive orchestra and lighting effects. Then as the second act forged ahead, disaster crept in.

Unnoticed by the audience, a light to the left of the stage area flashed, setting a painted drape on fire that swiftly carried the flame into the space above the performers, igniting the top of the fabric backdrops. Without warning, the blazing drapery crashed down, setting on fire the costume of at least one performer, who rushed offstage in a panic. As the stunned audience blindly rushed out, Eddie Foy attempted to stop the disorderly retreat. With mild success, Foy urged the crowd to remain calm. But when the actors opened a stage door to escape, the draft sent the existing fire blazing, and panic flared, too.

An asbestos curtain had been installed in the "fireproof" theater, but when crew members tried to lower it against the fire, it jammed several feet from the stage floor. Not long after the snafu, part of the stage collapsed. Then, to the horror of all present, the lights went out.

Twenty-seven exits had been designed for the Iroquois, but many had been locked against nonpaying guests. Others were hidden by curtains so as not to spoil the elegance. The stampede of people, the horror of the pitch-blackness, and the lack of available exits combined to create one of the grisliest scenes ever encountered by firefighters anywhere.

By the time they fought their way inside, past a main exit sealed shut by a seven-foot-high wall of corpses, not a living soul remained. Well over 500 people, most of them women and children, lay, trampled and asphyxiated, behind the main theater doors, doors that opened, incredibly, *inward.*

The Iroquois itself was a shambles of ashes and charred marble, the critically acclaimed "temple of beauty" turned chamber of horrors in a matter of minutes. Over the weeks that followed, more than two dozen with fire-related injuries would join the departed audience members, and hundreds would nurse injuries, some for a lifetime. The indictments that ensued against managers and officials who, in the rush to complete the theater, glossed over inspections and unfinished safety features, offered little consolation to the thousands who lost loved ones in the unspeakable tragedy.

Those who lived tried as best they could to blend back into the lives they had known. Scars, physical, mental, and emotional, made the attempt a brutal struggle. One North Center woman, an Iroquois organist, came away from the disaster alive, but with a face so badly marred that she wore a veil ever after along with the turn-of-the-century costumes she had worn before the fire. Known only as Mrs. Meyers, neighbors would see her well into the 1940s, keeping far from others, outfitted in her somber Gibson Girl attire. On rare daylight outings, she would pause frequently to touch up heavy makeup. In the evenings, neighborhood children followed her stealthily as she made her way, in the safe darkness, to window-shop at Broadway and Lawrence and recall the days when the bustle of the Loop was open to her.

Mrs. Meyers died in 1970, 67 years after the tragedy. With her went one of the last living witnesses to that devastating day on Randolph Street. Theater life there, however, would go on. Some time after the demolition of the Iroquois, the Oriental Theatre had been built on the same land. Decades passed, and after waning attendance at Loop theaters, the Oriental, too, was shuttered. A massive rehabilitation effort, inspired by Mayor Richard M. Daley's push for the renaissance of the old Randolph Street downtown theater district, threw open the doors on the old Oriental, sparkling again and re-named the Ford Center for the Performing Arts. Yet, while the doors all open outward, and state-of-the-art sprinkler systems stand at the ready, prepared to saturate the tiniest of sparks, something here remains unconvinced of the preparedness of this place.

The alley behind the Ford Center is the same alley that ran behind the ill-fated Iroquois in the waning days of 1903. Though rescuers found at the theater's front the unopening doors barricaded with bodies, the horror out back was, if possible, even worse:

> The rear alley was a smoking, flaming hell.
>
> . . . Firefighters heard the pounding behind iron-shuttered doors and windows and tried to wrench them open with axes and claw bars. Above them, the unfinished fire escape door suddenly flew open. People, many on fire, were pushed onto the platform that led nowhere but down. Body after body thudded onto the cobblestones.
>
> Another fire escape door was pried open and people were running down it when the door directly underneath was blown open by pent-up heat and gasses. Fire spewing from the door spiraled upward and engulfed people coming down the escape. Firefighters spread black nets, but few of the trapped saw them through the smoke. More jumped and survived only because their bodies were cushioned by those who had leaped before them.

Adding to the death toll in the alleyway were others, mostly women and children, who had attempted to crawl across a makeshift bridge extended by students and workers from the Northwestern University building located across the way, many tumbling to the pile of corpses below. When the mania was over, 125 bodies lay in the space that Chicagoans would forever call "Death Alley."

Today, the alley behind the fully restored Oriental Theatre/Ford Center for the Performing Arts is usually empty, its narrow passage maneuvered only by the occasional delivery truck, stagehand, or performer, or by a pedestrian grabbing a shortcut to a late appointment.

The void, however, may be deceiving.

Those who do find themselves in "Death Alley" never feel quite alone here, and never quite comfortable. Faint cries are half-heard in the constant gloom of this canyon-like passage; grips on the arm by unseen hands are not uncommon; and a pervasive chill, even in the deep heat of a Chicago summer, blesses each wanderer in here with an icy kiss.

Background information on the Iroquois Theatre fire of 1903 was provided by David Cowan, author of Great Chicago Fires. *Memories of Mrs. Meyers, the organist who survived, were kindly provided by her longtime North Center neighbors. The quotation on p. 240 is from Paul C. Ditzel's* Fire Engines, Fire Fighters *("The Iroquois theatre: 'absolutely fireproof'," p. 166).*

KEELER AVENUE HAUNTS

An Elusive Houseguest
Comes Out to Play

ALMOST COMMON IS THE sudden haunting of a house or other site when its owners decide to renovate, remodel, or otherwise alter the building's established appearance. Sometimes, a previous owner, resident, or even the builder himself will make his presence known after years or even generations of passive, invisible coexistence with the current tenants.

In Chicago's grand old neighborhoods, dormant hauntings like these are a very real part of upscale urban life, as couples and families seek to overhaul their under-maintained dwellings, often with curious consequences.

Sisters Roxanne and Michelle White grew up in a house in the city's Old Irving Park neighborhood. When the girls were 11 and 12 years old, respectively, their parents decided to initiate a simple home improvement project—the remodeling of the first-floor bathroom. Little did the couple know that the gesture would set off a surprising phenomenon: the drawing out of a long-gone playmate for their two adolescent daughters. Roxanne, now 14, remembers:

> It was early August in 1998. Our bathroom on the first floor
> was being remodeled. The workers remodeling were carrying in
> plywood and huge boxes of tile, and when I peeked in through the
> doorway, it looked as though the floor was ripped to shreds. My
> parents were told that we couldn't use that bathroom, so we used
> the nice bathroom in the basement. While the bathroom was bright
> and fairly clean, a normal bathroom, the rest of the basement was
> awful. It was dark and musty, and full of spiders. Altogether scary.
> If there was such a thing as the bogeyman to an 11-year-old, it
> could have easily resided in that basement.

The replacing of the floor in the bathroom was estimated to take about three days. On the first day, the workers pulled up the floor and found very old wooden planking underneath. They pulled it out and left.

It was the next morning, before the workers had arrived, that the first unusual thing happened. Mom, Dad, and I were in the kitchen making breakfast for ourselves. Mom was hunched over a book and a cup of coffee at the table. Dad was making toast, and I was having a banana when I heard footfalls behind me. I turned around, and my parents looked up. It sounded like my little sister, Griffin, running across our dining room.

Griffin's awake? my mom asked in surprise. I poked my head around the doorway and scanned the dining room. Empty. I turned back and said, *No one's there.*

Then what was that? Mom asked. Dad just looked perplexed. I left the kitchen and walked upstairs to my parents' room. I was curious. Sure enough, Griffin was in bed, sound asleep.

We all shrugged it off, figuring it was nothing, and went our separate ways: Dad to work, Mom to the post office with Griffin, my older sister, Michelle, and I at home. I called my best friend and made plans for her to hang out at my house that afternoon.

That day was scorching. The sun beat down and dried up the vegetable garden, as it had for weeks before. When my friend came over, we brought our tape player out into the backyard. Michelle put on a Jimi Hendrix tape, and we ran around, squirting each other with the hose and shrieking. Eventually, we got so hot and sweaty and tired that we decided to cool off in the basement bathroom. Michelle went upstairs to get dry towels, leaving my friend and me in the basement. We were gabbing, not paying much attention to anything, when suddenly the door slid open.

We both straightened up simultaneously. The door slid shut again. We stared at each other, our mouths hanging open like goldfish. After a brief moment of shock, I turned back to the door. The movements were changed; instead of fully opening and shutting, it was wiggling a little on its hinges. I began to doubt my judgment.

All right, Michelle, what— I stopped when I saw that there was no one outside the door. My friend was full of fear: her face had a sickly, greenish look to it.

Michelle came down the basement stairs, her sandals clicking with each step.

I brought some towels and a comb, she said, and then she caught sight of our faces.

What's wrong with you? she asked. I described the way the door had opened and shut. She gave us very mature, reassuring glances.

Look. Come here, she called as she knelt on the floor outside the door. I followed her. My friend refused to exit the bathroom, though. Michelle passed her hand to and fro, in front of the doorway.

See? There's a draft.

Could a draft make the door open and close like that? I believed her, though still skeptical. She didn't answer.

We all hurried upstairs. My friend was getting over her temporary fright, and now she was chatty again. We went for a walk around the neighborhood, had a mini-picnic on the front lawn, and walked my friend home. We came back to our house. Michelle went down into the basement, while I stayed outside. I really didn't want to see the door opening on its own again.

Michelle walked down the steps. Once she was at the bottom, she stopped and squinted into the darkness. She saw (in her own description) a flickering light, like the sun shining through the leaves on trees. The door to the basement was thick and wooden. There were no windows. So where was this light coming from? That was when I heard Michelle yelling for me.

I came running down the stairs at stopped at the bottom, next to Michelle. I saw something, too, though it wasn't the same as what Michelle saw. I think I perceived the whole experience as something different.

There was a strange shadow farther back in the basement. It was huge, formless, and pitch-black. But there was nothing big enough to cast a shadow like that. Also, how could there be any shadows if there was no light to cast shadows? And at that moment, I heard a little girl's voice. It said, *Do you want to talk to me?*

Michelle seemed a good deal calmer than me, though later she confided to me that she was terrified. She said, *Don't worry. We're not afraid of you. You're welcome here,* or something to that effect. I was scared out of my mind and was actually shaking.

Neither of us remembers exactly what we said.

Reassured by Michelle's words, I grew slightly calmer. Both of us began talking, simply about how we liked the ghost and that she was welcome anytime, because—although each of us perceived the overall experience differently—we both knew that this was a little girl, about five or six years old.

We continued talking comfortingly like this, then eventually Michelle said, *We'll be back later. Bye!* We backed up the stairs and closed the door.

That evening we went out to a restaurant for dinner. When we returned home, Michelle and I hesitated to wash up in the basement. It wasn't only what we'd seen earlier that scared us; the basement was just naturally creepy. We went down finally, straight to the bathroom and switched on the lights. We weren't quite so scared with the bright lights flooding the small room. I was washing my face, the water running, when I heard a sound. It was giggling! It sounded like a little girl was outside the room in the far part of the basement. I turned off the water and looked at Michelle. She looked at me. She'd heard it, too.

Michelle got up and we walked slowly to the door. She opened it, and the light flooded out into the basement.

Hello? Michelle called. There was no answer. I spoke then, to the girl.

Why don't we call you by some certain name, so you know when we're talking to you or talking to each other? Michelle nodded.

Is it all right if we call you Mary? I asked. No reply. I didn't really expect an answer anyway.

Okay, we're going upstairs now. Goodnight, Michelle called as I switched off the light and went upstairs.

We were sitting upstairs in our shared room, brushing our hair and changing into our pajamas. It was easy to be comforted in that room, because everything was softened by the lamplight, including the stuffed animals at the foot of Michelle's bed, which didn't really need softening! There was a big red bear, a couple of toy dogs, and a small fuzzy lamb. I went into the hallway to get a book, and when I came back, Michelle was looking at me suspiciously.

Where's my sheep? she demanded.

What sheep? I didn't take it, I said. *Go ahead, search me. What would I want with your sheep, anyway?*

We looked and looked for it, but we couldn't find it. We decided to look when it would be daylight out.

I woke up in the middle of the night for no reason. My digital clock glowed 3:17 A.M. I began to hear a faint sound, someone humming. It got gradually louder, but I still couldn't place the melody. It was unfamiliar, and the closest tune I can think of is "Greensleeves." I just lay there a moment, half-asleep, thinking, *Oh. Somebody's humming. Okay.* I turned over and fell asleep again.

Though I didn't know it, Michelle heard humming that night, too. She heard it long before I did. Now she says it sounded like some old-fashioned song, but familiar. After listening for a few seconds, she called, *Mom?* and the humming stopped.

The next morning, Michelle and I were heading to the basement to wash up (again). I was the first down the stairs, and as soon as the basement was in view, I stopped dead in my tracks. The sheep was lying in plain sight, on an overturned milk crate. At my side, Michelle laughed.

What? I asked.

Isn't it obvious? Mary had a little lamb. See?

I guess she liked the name, I said, all the while thinking, Did she take the lamb as a signal that she accepted her "name"?

That day, construction on the upstairs bathroom was finished, so we could use it again. Michelle and I still went downstairs to visit Mary, but she didn't seem to be there anymore. I guess she was happy that we accepted her, and so she just left. We have never seen anything from that particular ghost again.

When we told Mom and Dad about Mary, they tried to figure out who she was. My father thinks she was Mrs. Schultz, an old lady who lived here a long time ago. Her father built the house when she was a child. My mom thinks that it's impossible for an old lady to come back as a little girl. Michelle thinks that Mary died as a little girl in that house, not Mrs. Schultz.

We moved out of that house almost a year ago.

Michelle and Roxanne White related the story of Mary and her little lamb to the author in a written account in the spring of 2000.

EDGEWATER HOSPITAL HAUNTS

Author's photo.

Veteran Chicago cops still talk about the supernatural murder mystery that centered on the staff of this Ashland Avenue institution.

A Killer's Deed
Comes Back to Haunt

WHEN, **IN THE SPRING** of 1977, respiratory therapist Remy Chua saw co-worker Teresita Basa in the staff lounge of Chicago's Edgewater Hospital, Basa had been dead for more than a month.

On a bitter February night, Basa had been discovered by firefighters under a burning mattress in her Pine Grove Avenue apartment. She had been stripped of her clothing, and her legs were found spread apart, suggesting that Basa had been the victim of a random rape and murder, not unusual in the diverse and often dangerous North Side neighborhood. Yet, 23rd District police soon discovered that things were not as they seemed when they initially guessed at the character of Basa's killing. Forensics reports revealed that the 48-year-old Philippine native had been a virgin, and with no sign of forced entry, the police guessed that she had willingly let her murderer into her apartment. Still, with all alibis clean as could be, police were left with scant information to go on, and the case faded as new tragedies demanded department attention.

Basa's attacker would likely have gone free if not for Teresita's own *post mortem* intervention. After appearing to co-worker Chua on that extraordinary spring afternoon, Basa haunted her old colleague night and day. To the puzzlement and concern of husband Joe and hospital workers who had known Teresita, Chua began to inadvertently mimic Basa's behavior: sitting in her favorite cafeteria chair, using her employee locker, and exhibiting the vacant, melancholy appearance that had shadowed Basa's personality. As the months went by, Chua became more and more distant from her husband and co-workers, often drifting into trance-like states in which she would sing songs that had been Basa's favorites, later insisting that she hadn't said a word.

In addition to the strange transformation of her outward character,

Chua was experiencing an inner change as well. Increasingly, her nights were filled with dreams of her dead colleague, whose face hovered above Chua's through long, deep sleeps. When the visions of Basa were joined by another, that of an Edgewater Hospital orderly almost unknown to her, the frightened Chua began smelling smoke upon waking, an experience which often sent her out of bed and around the dark house, searching for the source of the fire. Though the nightmares, visual and olfactory, worsened, Chua's husband tried to console her, convinced that the horror of Basa's murder had been delayed in registering with Remy, and that she would soon get over the trauma of the experience and return to her normal state.

What happened next, however, was far from normal.

On a quiet afternoon at the Chua house, Remy was napping in the couple's bedroom while Joe made business phone calls in the kitchen. Suddenly, a blood-curdling scream rang through the house, obviously Remy's. When Joe entered the room in a panic, along with Remy's visiting parents, they found the bedroom freezing cold. Remy's mother would later claim that her hair had stood on end, a sure sign of a ghostly presence. Remy herself appeared to be sleepwalking, her arms outstretched and her eyes glassy. Falling backwards onto the bed, Chua began to speak in an alien voice, intoning that she was Teresita Basa.

Remy's family stood transfixed, absorbing "Teresita"'s message: *My killer is free—go to the police—tell them what happened to me. The orderly from the hospital murdered me. He came into my apartment and killed me.*

Addressing Joe, a doctor, "Teresita" implored him to use his status to convince detectives of the authenticity of the communication. Then the voice gave Joe a clue to the necessary evidence: the name of the orderly, a description of a cache of jewelry that the killer had stolen for his girlfriend, and the phone numbers of relatives who could identify the stolen pieces as Basa's own.

Stunned by the encounter, but despairing of help, Joe and Remy's parents ignored the pleas of the mysterious voice until, days later, a horrified Remy awoke with a start, screaming that she was burning. Again, the alien voice begged for help, and Joe, out of options and desperate for an end to his wife's terror, took his story to Detective Joe Stachula.

Stachula placed little faith in the story Joe Chua laid before him, but the veteran detective was used to success and instantly determined to give the case his best shot. Running the orderly's name for criminal records, Stachula discovered that the man in question had been arrested a number of times. Moreover, the families of deceased Edgewater Hospital patients had accused him of stealing jewelry from their dead relatives.

Bringing the orderly in for questioning, Stachula heard an alibi that his wife had been with him the night of the murder. When pressed, the suspect admitted that he had been friends with Basa, and that he had gone to her apartment that February night to fix her television set. Returning to his own place for some needed tools, he had not gone back as promised, remaining instead with his wife at home. When Stachula questioned the orderly's wife, she turned out to be a live-in girlfriend, a longtime fiancée who'd been given an heirloom-quality promise ring by her lover as a belated Valentine's gift. Returning to area headquarters with the suspect's girlfriend, Stachula called the phone numbers supplied by the "spirit voice" and found that they were those of Basa's cousins and closest acquaintances. Calling them in for questioning, Stachula watched the crowd easily identify the ring and a box of other jewelry as Teresita's possessions.

Though the orderly maintained that he had bought the ring and other baubles in a North Side pawn shop, he cracked when he saw his girlfriend enter the interrogation room. A lengthy and gruesome confession poured out and, two years later, the case went to trial. A hung jury sent the orderly back to a holding cell and, while awaiting a new trial, the suspect suddenly pleaded guilty to the crime he continued to deny, even after his earlier confession of murder.

Some say that an anonymous and undetectable cellmate may have pressured the suspect into a change of heart.

The author first learned of the murder of Teresita Basa and the incredible events that followed from veteran Chicago police officers. A short account of the incident is included in Richard Winer's Houses of Horror, *and a detailed account of the case may be found in* A Voice from the Grave.

ELMHURST LIBRARY HAUNTS

Photo by D. Cowan.

This stately village landmark shelters a bookloving phantom.

A Bookloving Ancestor
Refuses to Check Out

WHEN, IN THE LATE 1860s, Elmhurst resident Seth Wadham built a home for his family, little did he guess that this house, which he christened White Birch, would one day become the town's public library. Little, too, would he have believed the popular rumor that he himself haunts it.

From the 1880s to the early 1920s, the Wadham home title passed through a number of hands. In 1922 the Elmhurst Library moved its several-thousand-volume collection from a tiny room in the old Glos Building into Seth's old homestead.

In the late 1920s, fire damaged the north roof, and the building was rewired and redecorated. Previously, the library had occupied only the ground floor, but after the renovation, part of the second floor was opened for library business.

Despite the overhaul, by 1936, the Elmhurst Library faced serious space problems, and the building fund started an eight-month renovation, in hopes of making room for the ever-expanding collection, now numbering more than 17,000 volumes.

The frequent and major alterations to the library structure began in the 1950s to give rise to rumors regarding the haunting of the building, a typical consequence of extensive renovations. Patrons and employees reported unusual goings-on: books flying from the shelves of the stacks, or stacks of tomes carefully shelved by unseen hands; lights found on in the morning after evening closings; feelings of being watched.

When, in the 1960s, another expansion project was approved, frequenters of the library braced themselves for a fresh onslaught of ghostly activity. Reports did multiply as more and more patrons heard stories of the library's unpaid employee; soon the library was marked as haunted, a reputation that spread among west suburban bookworms and ghost lovers.

Today, electronic and other modern collections, thousands of additional volumes, and an ever-increasing clientele are making another, unprecedented expansion of the Elmhurst Library inevitable. This time, a new building may be the only way to make enough room for the future, leading some to wonder where Seth, who has lived in the building's attic since 1922, will go. Librarians, who joke about Wadham but credit his phantom to a creative librarian who invented the haunting years ago, say don't worry: the house's builder has been in his grave since his nineteenth-century passing.

But patrons know the truth. A dictionary falls to the floor for no reason; a reading lamp suddenly flickers on; invisible footfalls echo in an adjacent aisle. With a thoroughly modern future ahead, Elmhurst Library patrons are loath to give up their ghost.

The Elmhurst Library provided background information on the library and its alleged attic inhabitant.

Maxwell Street Haunts

Photo courtesy of the Chicago Public Library.

The world-famous Maxwell Street Market in the 1930s.

"The Old Red Ship"
and a Lady in Black

CHICAGO'S WELL-STORIED MAXWELL STREET neighbor-
hood has never been short on folklore. The jumble of life here has lived
harder than most Chicagoans, seeing the place through from its tough
days as the city's Jewish ghetto, to its glory days as urban marketplace
extraordinaire, to its modern hard times as rickety holdout of all that is
good and true in Chicago. Myths, too, are more monstrous here than in
the city's other environs, from the legend of the devil baby who showed
up in the early twentieth century on the doorstep of Jane Addams's
nearby Hull House to the rumored ravings of former prisoners from the
shuttered dungeon of the notorious Maxwell Street Police Station.

By the time it was glorified nationwide in the early 1980s, in the
opening frames of the popular TV crime drama *Hill Street Blues*, the
Maxwell Street Station (943 W. Maxwell Street) had already endured
nearly 100 years of notoriety in its own town. From its inception, it ruled
over the precinct the *Chicago Tribune* christened "Bloody Maxwell," a
turn-of-the-nineteenth-century name that would fit well into the twenty-
first. For this was "the crime center of the country," filled with
"[m]urderers, robbers and thieves of the worst kind." And in those days
of Eastern European immigration, and the later days of African-
American and Hispanic infusion, the Bloody Maxwell station was
known variously as "The Old Red Ship," "The Old Fortress," and "The
Rock of Gibraltar." Built to last in 1888, the red and gray stone building
towered above the incessant swarm of life here, staking a claim for good
at any cost in "the wickedest police district in the world."

Like the facts behind the beatings alleged to have occurred here
with alarming frequency until its closing in 1951, the ghosts of the 12th
District dungeon are hard to lay hands on. Despite their vagaries,

however, they are easy to believe in. The dungeon's history is rife with shock tales: the dozens of prisoners who "fell" down the two flights of marble steps to the front desk; the reported beatings on the kidneys with phone books; the sudden and numerous deaths of perfectly healthy inmates. Whether any of these stories are true, the living hell described by one prisoner was fact: 31 cells, four of them women's, were installed in the station's cellar during a surge in crime at the beginning of the twentieth century, during which officers at Maxwell wrote up a murder a day. For half a century, prisoners in the station's near-catacombs urinated, vomited, and bled into troughs dug from the floor, the refuse flowing under the cells of a dozen fellow convicts. Rats flourished. The walls grew black and blue with graffiti.

Though the allegations of "lower Maxwell" beatings were halted by the mid-century shutdown of the basement cells, rumors of the cells' continued use abounded, in and out of police circles. Though the station and the city denied such charges, the dungeon bars were sawed down to the floor sometime in the 1970s.

Though the Old Red Fortress has, like much of the Maxwell Street neighborhood, been consumed by the University of Illinois at Chicago, stories of its dungeon prevail, along with reports of bloodcurdling cries seeping from the basement windows. Also alive and well is another neighborhood mystery: a local legend known only as the Lady in Black.

Hailing from the earliest days of "Bloody Maxwell," as betrayed by her period clothing, a silent female phantom has been known to play both guardian angel and prophetess to unsuspecting citizens. The country was introduced to the kindly specter through television's *Unsolved Mysteries*, which documented the rescue of a motorcyclist in the Maxwell Street area by a mysterious black-clad woman who saved the stranger and vanished into thin air. Paramedics testified to the incident, adding to the credibility of the tale.

Similarly, in the late 1960s, a Chicago Police recruit encountered a mysterious woman outside a local eatery. The meeting would remain with him more than 30 years later:

> I was twenty years old. I was enrolled in the Chicago Police Academy, which was located near Maxwell Street and the Dan (Ryan) expressway. I had been attending the academy for several months and was taking lunch with two other academy students.

As we entered a small restaurant in this area, I remember a white lady dressed in all black clothes. Her dress reminded me of someone from the 1800s, and the reason I mentioned her color is because the area was basically a black neighborhood and seeing a white lady in this area made this individual encounter even stranger.

Now, as I stood in the entryway to the restaurant with my friends on either side of me, this Lady in Black came up to me and looked right into my eyes. Without a word or hand gesture or even a facial expression, she somehow communicated to me to hand her the pen and small note pad I had in my upper left hand shirt pocket. I did just that without knowing exactly why. She took the pen and note pad and wrote something into the note pad. Then she looked at me and shook her head in a gesture of no, no, no. She handed me the pen and note pad and left abruptly.

I looked into the note pad and noticed what she wrote: my name and my birth date. But then I also realized that it was in my own handwriting. I quickly turned to my friends and asked them, *Did you see what the lady just did?* They responded to my question as though I was crazy: *What lady?* They acted as if nothing unusual happened, and we went into the restaurant and had lunch.

Well, this strange little encounter stayed with me, and (because of it) I always felt that I would have to quit the Chicago Police Department someday.

I felt she was telling me to leave this career in order to save my life.

The author is greatly indebted to the author of the eyewitness account of Maxwell Street's Lady in Black, which was published in Dennis William Hauck's online newsletter, The Hauck Report, *of February 2, 1999 (Vol. 2 No. 2). Numerous attempts were made to contact the eyewitness for further information, without success, and so anonymity was used in respect of the witness. Those wishing to read more about the "Old Red Ship," the notorious Maxwell Street Police Station, will find no more colorful tale than Gary Moore's article, "The old red ship: a century of honor and mystery at the Maxwell Street police station," which appeared in the* Chicago Tribune Magazine *of March 15, 1998, from which the included quotations are extracted.*

HAND-ME-DOWN HAUNTS

Witness's photo.

Rescued from an uncertain fate, this adopted
artifact proved to have a life of its own.

A Garage Sale Find Makes a Lasting First Impression

LORI WARNER* IS NO stranger to the supernatural. Having lived in southwest suburban Midlothian for years, she has long been a neighbor of notorious Bachelors Grove Cemetery, the magical burial ground nestled into nearby Rubio Woods, which has garnered widespread fame thanks to its 50 years of ghostlore.

But Warner's acquaintance with the unexplained is even more intimate; for the past 20 years she has lived in a peculiar home whose phantoms take a variety of forms, including the untraceable smell of blueberry pie (see "Blueberry House Haunts," p. 21). Long before she got her own haunted house, however, Warner had another unsettling but solitary run-in with the Unknown, while she and her husband were living in a Midlothian apartment:

> I had just become a Christian. Now whether or not that has any bearing on the events that transpired I could only speculate.
>
> What happened was that I had purchased a crucifix from a garage sale. (The woman who had owned the home was going into a nursing home.) Although I was not particularly "Catholic," I was upset that the family wasn't sending the crucifix with her as I view such items as personal or belonging to a family. I suggested this to the people having the sale and, more or less, they told me not to worry, she didn't need it. So, I purchased it and took it home.
>
> I placed the crucifix over my dresser in our bedroom. Soon afterward, my husband and I went out. When we returned, he went into the bedroom and became very agitated, asking me how on earth had I burned the floor? I had no idea what he was talking about and went to look.

When I entered the room I saw that on the floor directly below the crucifix were three triangular shaped burns. By burns, I mean they were marks blackened and embedded into the wooden floor. The burns faced each other in a clover-shaped formation and were perfectly symmetrical. They resembled the front portion of an iron, but only the tip. Hence my husband's idea that I had somehow burned the floor.

Well, we placed our iron on the spots and discovered that, first of all, they did not match and, secondly, if the iron were to blame, it would have been virtually impossible to burn the floor with only the front of the iron, especially considering the depth of the burn. Lastly, I don't iron on the floor.

My husband immediately wanted the crucifix removed but, although I was frightened, I insisted that it was a symbol of God and that it should stay.

Considering the degree of the burns, I would assume that they, too, remain to this day, unless the boards of the floor were re-placed or carpeted over. We left that apartment shortly afterward and the crucifix came with us; we have had no more "problems" arise from it.

It hangs today in my living room over the doorway to the kitchen.

An alternate name has been used at the request of the witness, who shared with the author the story of the curious crucifix purchased at a garage sale in a written account in the summer of 2000.

GOLD COAST HAUNTS

Photo by Matt Hucke.

The mausoleum of Ira Couch near North Avenue in Lincoln Park,
on the grounds of the Chicago Historical Society, is the last
visible remnant of Chicago's City Cemetery.

Grave Problems in the Lap of Luxury

ON CHICAGO'S GOLD Coast, that exclusive lakefront enclave, ghosts are a dime a dozen, though not many are talked about by their ultra-chic flesh-and-blood housemates.

When, in 1885, Archbishop Patrick Feehan set up housekeeping in a lavish mansion on State Parkway, a large acreage surrounded the dwelling. For decades, the Chicago Gold Coast had kept its dead here, interred in the old City Cemetery just beyond North Avenue. When the question of disease threw lakefront residents into a panic, the cemetery was closed and the bodies relocated to outlying sites along the Chicago and North Western rail line: Catholics went to Calvary, on the border between Chicago and Evanston, a town directly north of the city limits. The others were buried in Rosehill, bordered today by Ravenswood, Peterson, Western, and Berwyn Avenues.

With the corpses gone, the abandoned expanse was open for suggestions. Though any of a million developmental fates might have befallen it, a wonderful one awaited. In 1868, much of the land became Lincoln Park. The rest was sold off for residential development. Yet, while the lakefront and its adjacent neighborhood would become beautiful over the next half century, little did the earliest squatters know that this area was destined to become one of the swankiest neighborhoods in America. Little, too, did they realize that bodies from the empty cemetery would continue to turn up here for the next 100 years.

Fourteen years after the opening of Lincoln Park, Potter Palmer, Chicago's most influential businessman of the day, moved into a million-dollar castle at 1350 N. Lake Shore Drive, fleeing the elite community of Prairie Avenue, south of the city center. In a short time, Palmer's former neighbors followed suit, and the old burial ground began to really glimmer. From then on, Chicago's old and new money would consider the Gold Coast as the ultimate in city living.

Many of the sumptuous residences that arose from this former swamp still stand today, relics of an age of overkill. Living in them are a number of descendants of those first Chicago "haves" and a host of relatively new millionaires as well. Though their origins may vary, many have at least two things in common: they're loaded, and they're haunted.

Since the neighborhood's earliest days, Gold Coasters settling down on Dearborn Parkway, State Parkway, and Astor Street have been aware of a sort of shadow population living with them in these haunts of the rich and famous (a population hailing, presumably, from the old City Cemetery) and the remains that, despite the cemetery's relocation, remained right here, often under the foundations of their houses.

After the first run-ins with partially decomposed corpses during the groundbreaking of the early homes and the hasty disposal of the evidence, residents complained of strange goings-on in their dream homes. As these hauntings arose time and again, would-be builders listened well. Soon, an unspoken understanding prevailed among future homeowners: when remains were unearthed, no expense or effort was spared in properly burying the grisly find.

Even today, this silent pact holds true. When, just recently, at the end of the twentieth century, a wealthy businessman began the total renovation of a grand old structure on State Parkway, he was hardly surprised at the discovery of an early team of contractors and well prepared with an old neighborhood solution. One worker explains that

> when the renovation of the elegant brownstone began, the
> basement floor had to be opened up for plumbing, electrical,
> and ventilation work. The job had to be dug by hand, by pick
> and shovel, and the men digging the trenches unearthed human
> remains.
>
> The general contractor on the job had a Native-American
> laborer, a very spiritual man. When the men working on the trench
> would disturb any remains, they were told to go upstairs and get
> this laborer, who would then come down and remove the remains
> to the side of the trench and say prayers over them.

A good background of the Gold Coast neighborhood is found in Chicago: City of Neighborhoods. *The account of the accidental excavation on State Parkway was provided to the author in the summer of 2000 in a written account by an anonymous worker.*

Tiffin Theater Haunts

Author's photo.

The grand, old Uptown Theatre has been, at least temporarily, spared from the wrecking ball. Other theaters, like the West Side's Tiffin, live on only in the happy—and haunting—memories of former theater-goers.

A Vanished Neighborhood Theater Shielded a Mysterious Specter

FROM FAST-PACED MIRACLES IN silent-era storefront nick-elodeons to contemporary dollar shows in the city's run-down palaces, Chicagoans have long demanded their movie fix. In fact, in the big small town of Chicago, the neighborhood movie houses ruled the social world of generations of teenagers who flocked to local theaters on Saturday night.

It should not surprise, then, that in Chicago some of our most notorious haunts call the box office home. It was after a hot July night showing of *Manhattan Melodrama* that Public Enemy No. 1 John Dillinger took the FBI's fatal bullet in an alleyway just steps from Lincoln Avenue's Biograph Theater and became one of the city's favorite phantoms: a misty figure who causes cold spots and creepy feelings in so-called "Dillinger's Alley." Not too far from the Biograph, the former caretaker of the Music Box Theatre, a successfully revitalized art and revival film house, makes his ethereal rounds as ever. A mysterious curl of smoke from under the screen curtain is said to bear nightly witness to the death of an arsonist employee who trapped himself in a fire of his own making at the Tivoli Theater in Downers Grove. And some South Siders believe that the sidewalk in front of the old Brighton Theater bears ghostly impressions of the ill-fated, adolescent Grimes sisters, who saw their last Elvis Presley movie here in 1956 before disappearing for a winter month, only to be found frozen to death off German Church Road in suburban Western Springs.

Lifetime Chicago resident Dina Nardo is not alone, then, in her special understanding of the magic of the movies. As a girl growing up near the Tiffin Theater at North and Karlov Avenues, Nardo discovered that the stars on screen were not the only unreal characters to be found at her neighborhood movie house. During her years as a patron and, later, an employee of the Tiffin, she experienced the theater's rumored wraith twice:

> The ladies' washroom was located in the basement of the Tiffin. Sometime during 1970, during a visit to the theater, I had gone down to the bathroom with my friend and was waiting outside the stall for her to finish. There was a steel door at the end of the toilet room which opened into the building's boiler room. The door was open on this occasion and out of curiosity I went and looked into the boiler room. There was a recessed pit where two tanks stood up on steel legs. You could see underneath them, and they were placed end to end with about a 4-foot opening between them. When I looked at the tanks I saw a man in a black coat or cloak with a black, fedora-style hat. I couldn't make out facial features; it seemed the face was in dark shadow. He seemed to be looking towards the doorway where I was standing and I immediately started yelling for my friend to hurry up because there was a peeping tom looking into the women's washroom. Just as she was coming out of the stall he seemed to float sideways behind one of the standing tanks. I could not see any legs showing under the tank, and that's when I realized he was not a normal man.
>
> The figure had seemed solid, not transparent. Until I saw no legs under the tank, I thought I was looking at a real person. We ran upstairs and found the theater manager. I don't recall her name, but she was a middle-aged woman whom the kids all called "the Eagle." I told her what I'd just seen and she was very adamant in telling me that I was mistaken. It was just my imagination, she stated, and I shouldn't mention it to anyone.
>
> Four years later I saw the same figure again, and it moved in the exact same way: standing between the boilers for a few seconds and then disappearing behind them. This time I saw it because I was coming into the actual basement to use a small washroom there that served the Sweet Shop, an ice cream parlor which occupied the corner of the theater building and shared a common basement. As I came down the staircase with two friends, there it was again. It was just moving from the middle to behind a boiler. We turned and ran back up the stairs.
>
> I went to work at the Tiffin when I was sixteen, and I worked there for two years. However, I never saw the ghost again. It became somewhat of an obsession with me though, and I would

question the other employees, asking if they'd ever seen anything strange in the show. I personally found three other people who'd seen the same thing I had and also heard from the manager's daughter that her mother had witnessed it, too.

There was one other strange thing about the theater. Behind the screen there was a staircase which led up three flights to a fan circulation room. On the second-floor landing, there was a small room which was closed off by a caged and locked door. I think the room held some kind of electrical meters. The odd thing about this area, besides the eerie fact that it was lit by a red bulb, was that it was always freezing cold at the entrance to the room. There was no duct work or air-conditioning vents in that area, and no one could explain why it was always cold, but I went past it one day during a summer heat wave, and it was enough to raise goose bumps on my arms.

Dina Nardo provided her account of the Tiffin Theater in a written testimony to the author in the spring of 1998.

FREMD HIGH HAUNTS

Author's photo.

Don't be fooled by the modern face of this north suburban high school,
where old-fashioned phantoms find comfort among their peers.

The Unenrolled

THE KIDS AT PALATINE'S William Fremd High School are no strangers to the paranormal. After all, this is Cuba Road country, and that eerie old highway has been hosting abundant ghosts and their accompanying adolescent hijinks for decades. The freshmen entering first-year Fremd are thus ready for a few double-dares of the ghostly variety, when the last Friday bell rings, and the weekend nights stand wide open for adventure.

While more than willing to seek out haunting legends after hours along Cuba Road and in the road's infamous White Cemetery, what these students are unprepared for is the prospect of a disembodied classmate, a campus phantom bold enough to show itself during everyday class time, when decent spirits are reclining in their graves, preferably far from the halls of academe. Yet here at Fremd, not one, not two, but *three* such spirits try to blend into the sea of senior high-schoolers. Among record numbers of honors students and award-winning athletes, a couple of low-key co-eds do their own thing, unhampered by bells, exams, or the threat of detention.

Good thing. One of Fremd's mysterious students is a noisy ne'er-do-well said to haunt the school's Kolze Auditorium, a critic who comically flips the seats up and down and plays with the lights during dress rehearsals. Several students and teachers report having had spotlights shined on them when the tech booth was empty and locked, and a longtime director attests to the peculiar "spirit" of Kolze with similar accounts of annoying antics.

A second phantom roams the school, as teachers, students, and staff have reported eerie goings-on in all corners of the campus. Room 122-S is a favorite haunt; faculty members have heard sighs coming from nowhere while typing in the room. Visitors to the faculty study have wondered at the rustle of unseen papers. And in the fall of 1999, a pneumatic machine turned itself on in the tech lab, making a student teacher's skin crawl.

Though most of the events at Fremd High School are credited to anonymous ghosts, the identity of one Fremd phantom is sadly well-known. Swim team members have been reporting strange experiences in the school's pool and locker rooms since the late 1970s, when a freshman swimmer died of a heart attack after swimming several laps. Since the tragedy, team members have from time to time spotted a school-issue bathing suit floating in the pool and lying in the locker room. Those who try to turn the suit in find that it never quite makes it to the lost and found. Others are startled by the slamming of lockers by unseen hands. And divers claim that the water feels colder at the spot where the girl died; many swimmers avoid going near the accident site.

While skeptics pooh-pooh the story of Fremd's haunted pool, a number of faculty members join swimmers in insisting on the haunted nature of the facilities. Over the years, several of Fremd's swimming coaches have reported early to work, unlocking the pool and locker rooms and preparing for the gym classes and team practice. Switching on the lights over the pool, more than one coach has been greeted with an unnerving vision: an ethereal, violet haze that hangs over the water a moment—then dissolves, like the night itself, into memory.

The students, faculty, and staff of William Fremd High School were enormously helpful in offering for publication the details of their haunted campus. In particular, student Isabelle Burtan contributed the article "Ever feel prickly things on the back of your neck?" which appeared in the school's Viking Logue, *November 19, 1999. The story of the swimmer's death was told by student reporters Lauren Lindvig and Jill Naumes in "Fremd tragedy spawns ghostly rumors," which appeared in the same edition.*

63RD STREET HAUNTS

From the author's collection.

The Columbian Exposition proved a fertile hunting
ground for a prolific turn-of-the-century killer.

Black Cloud
over White City

LONG BEFORE NAMES LIKE Heirens, Speck, and Gacy blackened the pages of Chicago history, a native New Hampshire man made the city by the lake synonymous with sheer horror.

When, in 1887, Herman W. Mudgett (alias H.H. Holmes) was hired as a shopkeeper in a drugstore in Chicago's Englewood neighborhood, he had been missing for two years. Still a very young man, the not quite 30-year-old Holmes had already substantially ruined his life. About a decade earlier, he had married local girl Clara Lovering and settled down in New York for a time, where he worked as a schoolteacher before hearing the call of higher education. Holmes moved with Clara to Michigan, where he began medical school. The couple's time together was brief, however. Holmes sent his young wife home to her New Hampshire family; soon after, he was thrown out of school for stealing cadavers from the college anatomy lab and criminally charged for using them in insurance scams.

A year later Holmes was hired in Englewood, and his boss, a woman by the name of Holden, went missing herself. Though family members, friends, and fellow businesspeople were alarmed, Holmes explained that Holden had decided to move to California and had sold the business to him.

Holmes wasted no time in finding a second wife, ignoring the fact that his pending divorce from Clara was stuck in the legal system and, thus, not final. His new fiancée, Myrtle Belknap, was the daughter of North Shore big shot John Belknap. Two years after their wedding, Belknap left Holmes. Their marriage had been an odd one at best; Myrtle lived in Wilmette with her family while Holmes continued to live on the city's South Side.

After his second wife's walkout, Holmes began construction of an enormous house on the property he'd purchased across the street from his store at 63rd and Wallace Streets. With money from further insurance scams, Holmes raised his Englewood castle to awesome heights. The triple-story wonder contained 60 rooms, trap doors, hidden staircases, windowless chambers, laundry chutes accessed from the floors, and a stairway that led to a precipice overlooking the house's back alley.

In only a year, the Holmes Castle was completed, and its owner sent out word that many of its plentiful rooms would be available to out-of-town visitors to the Columbian Exposition. And so the horror began.

Detectives and later scholars guessed that an untold number of the fair's attendees met gruesome ends at the hands of Holmes in the castle he built as a giant torture chamber. It was later discovered that the building contained walls fitted with blowtorches, gassing devices, and other monstrosities. The basement was furnished with a dissecting table and vats of acid and lime. Alarms in his guest rooms alerted Holmes to escape attempts. Investigators believe that many were kept prisoner for weeks or months before being killed by their diabolical innkeeper.

Along with his hotel of horrors, Holmes had other ways of attracting victims. Placing ads in city papers, he offered attractive jobs to attractive young women. Insisting on the top-secret nature of the work, the location, and his own identity, he promised good pay for silence. In the competitive world of turn-of-the-century Chicago, there were many takers.

Far from satiated, Holmes advertised for a new wife, luring hopeful and destitute girls with his business stature and securing their trust with what must have been an irresistible charm.

After disposing of many potential employees and fiancées in his chambers of terror, Holmes decided to seriously find another mate. In 1893, he proposed to Minnie Williams, the daughter of a Texas realty king. Williams shared Holmes's violent nature and lawless attitude. The same year they met, Williams killed her sister with a chair. Her understanding, empathic fiancé dumped the body into Lake Michigan.

Longtime Holmes employees Julia Connor and her daughter, Pearl, were distraught at the news that their boss would be taking a new wife. Julia had been smitten with Holmes at the expense of her own marriage, and she and Pearl had worked with their employer to pull off a number of his insurance swindles. Not long after objecting to the coming union,

Julia and Pearl disappeared. When Julia's husband, Ned, came calling for them, Holmes told him that his family had moved to another state. In reality, Julia's alarm over Holmes's imminent marriage stemmed not from mere longing, but from the fact that she was pregnant with his child. Her death was the result of an abortion that Holmes had performed himself. Stuck with Pearl as an annoying witness, he poisoned the child.

It gets worse.

In 1894, the Holmeses went to Colorado with an Indiana prostitute in tow. Georgianna Yoke had moved to Chicago to start afresh and had answered one of Holmes's marriage ads in a local paper. Introduced as Holmes's cousin, Minnie saw in Yoke what Holmes saw: a girl with wealthy parents and a substantial inheritance awaiting her. In Denver, Minnie witnessed her husband's marriage to Yoke, and from there the trio went to Texas, transferred Minnie's property to Holmes, and conducted a few assorted scams. Not long after, the group returned to Chicago and Minnie, not Georgianna, went the way of Holmes's victims. Around the same time, Holmes's secretary, Emmeline Cigrand, was literally stretched to death in the Castle basement along with her visiting fiancé.

Finally, in July, 1894, Holmes was arrested for mortgage fraud. Though his third wife sprung him with their dirty bail money, Holmes had used his short time behind bars to launch yet another scam. Holmes planned to run a big insurance fraud at the expense of early accomplice Ben Pitezel, who had served time for one of their swindles while Holmes had walked away. Hoping to eliminate the possibility of Pitezel's squealing on their earlier capers, Holmes planned to get richer by rubbing the man out. With a shyster lawyer in tow, Holmes killed Pitezel in his Philadelphia patent shop after taking out an insurance policy on Pitezel's life.

When Holmes neglected to pay a share of the winnings to his old cellmate, Marion Hedgepeth (who had helped him plan the swindle), Hedgepeth turned in Holmes's name to a St. Louis cop, who made sure the tip got to Pinkerton agent Frank Geyer.

While Geyer dug up the dirt on Holmes, Holmes was digging graves for fresh victims. After Pitezel's death, Holmes had told his widow, Carrie, that some of Ben's shady dealings had been found out, and that he had therefore gone to New York incognito. Holmes then took Carrie and the Pitezel children under his dubious care. The family did not know their husband and father was dead.

While on the road with Georgianna and the remaining Pitezels, Holmes decided to send Carrie back east to stay with her parents. The Pitezel children were left in the hands of Holmes, who first killed Carrie's son, Howard, in an abandoned Indiana house, and then gassed her daughters after locking them in a trunk while the group was staying in Toronto.

Next, Holmes returned to his first wife Clara and, after explaining that he had had amnesia and mistakenly married another woman, was forgiven.

Whatever devilish plans Holmes had for his first love were thwarted when he was charged with insurance fraud. Holmes pleaded guilty while Frank Geyer searched the castle with police. What they found was astounding: the torture devices, the homemade gas chambers, the shelves of poison and dissection tools, the vats of lime and acid; all revealed the true criminality of the man being held for mere fraud. Evidence of the purpose of the grim house was easy to find: a ball of women's hair was stuffed under the basement stairs, Minnie's watch and dress buttons remained in the furnace, bits of charred bone littered the incinerator. Through the hot summer of 1895, crews worked to unearth and catalog all of the building's debris. Then, in late August, the Murder Castle burned to the ground in a mysterious fire, aided by a series of explosions. A gasoline can verified arson, but no one could tell if it was one of Holmes's many adversaries or the man himself that had done it.

Holmes was sentenced to death in Philadelphia, where he had killed his old accomplice. On May 7, 1896, he was hanged, to the relief of a nation and, particularly, Chicago, the city that had unknowingly endured the bulk of his insanity. Some claimed that at the moment of his hanging, Holmes cried out that he was the notorious London butcher, Jack the Ripper. Others swear that when Holmes's neck snapped, a bolt of lightning struck the horizon on the clear spring day.

The fact that Holmes remained alive with a broken neck for nearly 15 minutes after the execution fueled the belief that his evil spirit was too strong to die. Rumors of a Holmes curse abounded during the months and years that followed. Dr. William Matten, a forensics expert who had testified against Holmes, soon died of unexplained blood poisoning. Next, Holmes's prison superintendent committed suicide.

Then, the trial judge and the head coroner were diagnosed with terminal diseases. Not much later, Frank Geyer himself fell mysteriously ill. A priest who had visited Holmes in his holding cell before the execution was found beaten to death in the courtyard of his church, and the jury foreman in the trial was mysteriously electrocuted. Strangest of all was an unexplained fire at the office of the insurance company that had, in the end, done Holmes in. While the entire office was destroyed, untouched were a copy of Holmes's arrest warrant and a packet of photos of Holmes himself.

The eerie string of Holmes-related deaths stretched well into the twentieth century, ending with the 1910 suicide of former employee Pat Quinlan who, many believed, had aided Holmes in his evil enterprises at the Murder Castle. Those close to Quinlan told reporters that the death had been long in coming; for years, they said, Quinlan had been haunted by his past life with Holmes, plagued with insomnia, driven at last to the edge and over. Some still say that it was Holmes himself that had haunted the boy and that the Monster of 63rd Street had finally gone away, taking with him the one person who could reveal all the secret horrors of Holmes's brutal heart.

While the Murder Castle is long gone from the Englewood landscape where H.H. Holmes once walked, his evil spirit seems to inspire the bad seeds scattered in his old neighborhood. While the working-class and the woefully poor struggle to make a life here, others continue Holmes's gruesome tradition, carrying out the serial murders and random slayings that have long plagued the South Side Chicago neighborhood and its bordering areas. Those Englewood residents familiar with the area's dark history may pause at the corner of 63rd and Wallace and wonder about one man's legacy. Chilled by half-remembered rumors and all-too-real headlines, they may hurry home, looking behind and listening, remembering the old neighborhood and the secrets it keeps.

The tale of the "Monster of 63rd Street" is a classic Chicago horror story. A wonderfully detailed account of Herman Mudgett's deadly life and legacy can be found in Troy Taylor's Haunted Illinois.

STREETERVILLE HAUNTS

Author's photo.

The John Hancock Building was revealed by one
Streeterville native to be a dreadful Pandora's box.

Sick Buildings, Satanists, and a Devil of a Curse

THE STORY OF THE haunting of the Streeterville neighborhood is a tale unlike the others. Here is not folklore about mere ghosts and the tragedies that bore them, though these abide here, too. Rather, the enigma of Streeterville owes itself to the truly arcane, to the ancient Magick and its practitioners, both foolish and for real. It is a tale as old as the city itself, and at least as complex and colorful. It begins at Chicago's threshold, where it also ends, winding from a madcap marauder to a self-styled Satanist, and it goes something like this:

When Chicago was young, in the days before the Fire, one of the city's many entrepreneurs was a ragtag, ex-Civil War soldier named George Wellington Streeter, who was bored of military duty and began instead a varied career as circus barker, steamboat helmsman, and everything in between. Gracing Chicago with his arrival in 1886, Streeter resurrected his former title of "Captain" and bought a decrepit schooner, the *Reutan*, which he ran between Chicago and Milwaukee for anyone brave enough to board it. When, after arriving in Milwaukee after one trip, a violent storm forced his passengers to take the train back to Chicago, Cap Streeter and wife Maria braved the weather alone, sailing near-blindly toward Chicago and, ultimately, running aground on the land of N. Kellogg Fairbank, a wealthy and kindly businessman who granted the Streeters permission to remain on the property until their boat could be repaired.

Kellogg's benevolence led to his duping by the opportunistic Streeter, who promptly built a makeshift cottage where Northwestern University's lakefront campus stands today. Setting up shop among the legitimate businessmen of the Tremont Hotel at Lake and Dearborn Streets, he sold, piece by piece and to eager takers, "his" land in the self-styled "Deestrict of Lake Michigan," a "territory" governed, he claimed, by Streeter himself.

Simultaneously, Potter Palmer, then king of Chicago business and culture, had been attempting to create a newly posh residential area, superior to the Prairie Avenue district and crowned by Palmer's own lakefront mansion. Incensed that Streeter's shantytown was ruining his dream, Palmer and his cronies made one attempt after another to evict the grubby land-grabber in vain. Police officers entering the squatter's "property" were greeted by the shotgun-wielding Streeter, who was backed by wife Maria's nasty resourcefulness. On one occasion, she threw a pot of boiling water on a group of officers as they led her husband away. Streeter wriggled free, retrieved his rifle, and was back in charge in no time.

These exchanges continued right through the turn of the century. In the spring of 1900, 500 police officers marched on "Streeterville" to take the Captain once and for all, but an army of fellow squatters ran them off, stoning and clubbing them.

In 1921, Cap Streeter died of pneumonia, ending his fight for recognition of the Streeterville District as his own, but not before repaying the city for the evil it had done him in trying to take his land away. Recognizing that with his own death, his beloved territory would pass into enemy hands, he cursed the land forever, warning that no peace would come to those who would live and work on it.

Streeter's curse would take on very real dimensions. For nearly 40 years after his death, the courts were inundated with suits against the lakefront property owners, beginning with an action brought by Cap's second wife, Elma, who in 1924 filed a claim of one billion dollars against no less than 1,500 of Chicago's lakefront elite. Other Streeterville residents followed her lead; the last of the suits was not dismissed until 1940.

In the decades following the end of the legal battles, Streeterville began to flesh out its destiny as the glitzy commercial and residential hub of modern Chicago. Skyscrapers grew up on either side of Michigan Avenue, whose prestige had stretched north across the river from the world-famous Boul Mich to embrace the newer Magnificent Mile, which ended, or began, depending on perspective, in Streeterville. These were happy days for the neighborhood, whose swift development and increasing prestige seemed to herald the end of the squatter's spell. The highly-polished door of the new Streeterville seemed closed forever on the curse of the captain.

No way.

In 1968, Skidmore, Owings and Merrill's fantastic office-and-apartment complex, the John Hancock building, was completed, rising 1,100 feet into the Streeterville sky, and, some say, reopening the door for the old curse in a very real way.

Born on the site where the building would stand, Anton Szandor LaVey came into the world sophisticated, growing swiftly into a prodigious youngster, particularly gifted in music. After a varied string of careers, he gained himself quick and lasting fame when, on Walpurgisnacht, 1966, he shaved his head and founded the Church of Satan. Considered a crackpot, devil-worshipping sensationalist by most observers, LaVey was in fact a refined and personable philosopher who made a religion out of being human. Satan is, in LaVey's philosophy, the individual will. As humans, we are born to follow where our will, or nature, leads us: to actions as diverse and as natural as the unequivocal love of children and animals and the annihilation of those who do us wrong. Of course, Satanism is not only about the normal rules of life. Its charm lies, as with all religions, in the esoteric power it seeks to harness.

Like all priests, LaVey searched long and hard for the places where ethereal power might enter the human realm. Drawing on his early exposure to the works of horror novelist H.P. Lovecraft, he turned to arcane ideas for revelations about the sources and control of unearthly power. In a now-classic insight, LaVey incorporated the "strange angles" written of by Lovecraft and the "negative architecture" described in an obscure essay called *Houses That Kill* into an intriguing idea, formulating the Greater and Lesser Laws of the Trapezoid. According to these laws, certain angles that are harmful to most people could be beneficial to those who understand the way they work. The places where we work, if "off-kilter," can profoundly affect our lives. The more that a building's angles deter from the common, proper, box-like shape, the more prone we are to an architecture-inspired madness. The "not quite right" aspect of much modern architecture, then, becomes a sort of gateway for the chaotic forces of nature. Putting stock in LaVey's laws, one might reasonably credit much of the insanity of the modern world to the buildings in which it lives. Witness, too, the talk of "sick buildings" in the modern metropolis, which are blamed for a variety of brief and terminal illnesses, both physical and mental.

In Chicago, a haven for progressive architects, LaVey's philosophies run amok, nowhere more rampantly than on the site of his own birth, up and down the "not quite right" halls of the trapezoidal Hancock building. Here, one may gather much wood for LaVey's fire in the controversial, unsettled lives of many of its celebrated residents (among them Jerry Springer, Andrew Greeley, and the late Chris Farley) and in the unexplained actions of some of its lesser-known tenants, most notably Lorraine Kowalski who, in 1971, supposedly pushed herself through two quarter-inch panes of glass in her 90th-floor apartment, falling to her death on the sidewalk below. The suicide baffled investigators, who determined that a woman of Kowalski's slight stature could never have mustered the 280 pounds of force necessary to shatter that window.

Not in a proper building, anyhow. But in the Hancock, with the forces of nature running wild and at the ready, stranger things could happen—and do.

The curse of Cap Streeter is a classic Chicago legend with many versions. A succinct variety is found in June Skinner Sawyers's Chicago Sketches, *and a* Chicago Days *piece on Cap Streeter features some of the* Chicago Tribune*'s wonderful period photos of the the man, his infamous vessel, and his devoted wife. The late Anton LaVey's life story is chronicled by* The Secret Life of a Satanist; *his own Law of the Trapezoid is discussed in a number of his own works, including the curiously insightful and disturbingly rational* Devil's Notebook, *a collection of his essays.*

Appendix: On Your Own

Reprinted from *Chicago Haunts: Ghostlore of the Windy City* (Lake Claremont Press, 1997).

Self-Tours for the Self-Assured

HOPEFULLY, IT HAS BEEN made evident that nearly every part of the Chicago region harbors a dim but distinguished host of haunts. For the would-be ghosthunter, then, plotting an afternoon or evening of investigation should not be a difficult task. Nonetheless, the wise will bear in mind a few common-sensical precautions:

FOREST PRESERVES are just that: natural wooded areas that come complete with all the dangers of the natural environment—plus a sizeable population of undesirables that frequents them. Enjoy and explore, but go in a group and during the day, unless you're prepared to defend yourself against both seamy strangers and the notorious Forest Preserve District Police, neither of whom will welcome you warmly.

PRIVATE HOUSES are private homes. Drive by for a quick look at reportedly haunted properties, but never, ever ring a bell or approach a resident on their property. If they wanted an investigator, they would have called one.

MUSEUMS are for learning—but usually not about ghosts. If your ghosthunting brings you to a museum, step carefully. Pay the normal entrance fee and join the offered tour. Take photos as allowed. Show interest in the surroundings and exhibits. When your tour is finished, wait for a time when you can speak privately with your guide or with a guard, who will likely appreciate your discretion in asking about the site's alleged paranormality.

CHURCHES do not exist for the sake of ghosthunting. Visit these sanctuaries for a service or drop in before or after for a bit of silent observation. If you wish to take photographs, ask permission of an usher or caretaker first. Likewise, rectories are private homes. Do not ring doorbells with the intention of grilling the priests or receptionist on the nuances of their local haunting.

SCHOOLS. Elementary and high schools are off-limits, due to safety laws. Colleges and universities, however, are often unsecured. Stroll the halls of the public buildings, being careful not to disturb classes or employees. Steer clear of residence halls; these too are private homes. If you are at all in doubt about whether you may access an area, play it safe: ask a security guard or administrator.

BARS & RESTAURANTS are places of business. Patronize them. After enjoying your drinks or dinner, ask your bartender or waitperson if they've heard about the haunting of the site. Find out if you can speak to the manager or owner as well.

CEMETERIES are sacred, and the managements of many are understandably chagrined by the queries of ghosthunters. In particular, the Catholic Cemeteries of Chicago are adamantly anti-ghost. If you're looking for a haunted site, don't mention the haunting. Use a proper name and ask to be directed to the lot number of the deceased. Drive carefully and walk softly. Take photographs discreetly. Never try to linger past closing time.

GROUP TOURS FOR THE LILY-LIVERED

A number of organized tours are available to those interested in the Chicago area's haunted history. Though some are held only seasonally—that is, in the weeks surrounding Halloween—some are conducted year round. As October approaches, watch local weekend sections of the newspapers for additional tours by other local investigators like Howard Heim and Norman Basile. Call for availability and reservations.

EXCURSIONS INTO THE UNKNOWN are conducted by Ghost Research Society president, Dale Kaczmarek, and originate in southwest suburban Oak Lawn. For information, write Mr. Kaczmarek at P.O. Box 205, Oak Lawn, IL 60454-0205; or call (708) 425-5163. Or visit the GRS Web site at *www.ghostresearch.org.*

SUPERNATURAL RESEARCH TOURS with Supernatural Occurrence Studies are specifically designed for small groups (2–10 people) and involve participants first-hand in research and evidence collection at a variety of classic and SOS-exclusive haunted sites around Chicagoland. Visit the the SOS Web site at *www.sos-chicago.com*.

HAUNTED?

To request on investigation of an active private site—your home, office or business—or to report Chicago-area paranormal phenomena, contact:

SUPERNATURAL OCCURRENCE STUDIES, a Chicago-based research team, offers haunting confirmation, consultation, and explanation through the use of standard photography and recording equipment, heightened awareness to strange energy, new-school theories and methods, historical research, and a healthy sense of skepticism.
Contact Dave Black, SOSChicago@msn.com
www.sos-chicago.com

THE GHOST HUNTERS SOCIETY, based in the Chicago's northern suburbs, utilizes a state-of-the art computer system in tracking paranormal activity.
Contact Mike Komen, Poltermike@worldnet.att.net

THE GHOST RESEARCH SOCIETY, based in the southwest suburbs, utilizes various methods—including psychics' assessments—in conducting investigations as part of its membership activities.
Contact Dale Kaczmarek, (708) 425-5163
DKaczmarek@ghostresearch.org
www.ghostresearch.org

> **If you would like to discuss a current haunting or other paranormal occurrence, or if you have a personal account of a past experience that you would like to have considered for a future edition of *Chicago Haunts*, please write the author in care of Lake Claremont Press.**

BIBLIOGRAPHY

Angle, Paul M., ed., *The Great Chicago Fire (described by eight men and women who experienced its horrors and testified to the Courage of its Inhabitants)*. Chicago: Chicago Historical Society, 1971.

Barton, Blanche. *The Secret Life of a Satanist*. Feral House, 1992.

Brown, Slater, *The Heyday of Spiritualism*. New York: Hawthorn Books, 1970.

Clearfield, Dylan, *Chicagoland Ghosts*. Thunder Bay Press, 1997. Eerdmans Publishing Company, 1995.

Cowan, David. *Great Chicago Fires*. Chicago: Lake Claremont Press, 2001.

Enright, Richard T., *Capone's Chicago*. Lakeville, MN: Northstar Maschek Books, 1987.

Griffin, Dick and Rob Warden, eds., *Done in a Day: 100 Years of Great Writing from the* Chicago Daily News. Chicago: Swallow Press, 1977.

Guiley, Rosemary Ellen, *The Encyclopedia of Ghosts and Spirits*. New York: Facts on File, 1992.

Hecht, Ben, *1001 Afternoons in Chicago*. Chicago: University of Chicago Press, 1992.

Holli, Melvin G. and Peter D. Jones, *Ethnic Chicago: A Multicultural Portrait*. Grand Rapids, MI: William B. Eerdmans Publishing Company, 1995.

Huxley, Aldous, *The Doors of Perception* and *Heaven and Hell*. New York: Harper & Row, 1990.

James, William, *The Will to Believe*. n.p.: Dover Publications, 1956.

LaVey, Anton S. *The Devil's Notebook*. Feral House, 1992.

Lindberg, Richard, *Return to the Scene of the Crime*. Nashville, TN: Cumberland House, 1999.

Mercado, Carol and O.A. *A Voice from the Grave*. Oak Park, IL: Carolando Press, 1979.

Miller, Donald S., *City of the Century: The Epic of Chicago and the Making of America*.

Moore, R. Laurence, *In Search of White Crows: Spiritualism, Parapsychology and American Culture.* New York: Oxford University Press, 1977.

Pacyga, Dominic A. and Ellen Skerrett, *Chicago: City of Neighborhoods.* Chicago: Loyola University Press, 1989.

Sawyers, June Skinner, *Chicago Sketches.* Chicago: Loyola Press, 1995.

Scott, Beth and Michael Norman, *Haunted Heartland.* New York: Warner Books, 1985.

Steiger, Brad, *Psychic City: Chicago, Doorway to Another Dimension.* Garden City, NY: Doubleday & Company, 1976.

Swanson, Stevenson, *Chicago Days: 150 Defining Moments in the Life of a Great City.* Chicago: Cantigny First Division Foundation, 1997.

Taylor, Troy, *Haunted Illinois.* Alton, IL: White Chapel Productions Press, 1999.

Tisler, C.C., *Starved Rock: Birthplace of Illinois.* n.p.: 1956.

Waldrop, Frank C., *McCormick of Chicago.* Englewood Cliffs, NJ: Prentice-Hall, 1966.

Index

A

Abenaki tribe, 116
Addams, Jane, 263
Adler Planetarium, 57, 231
Algren, Nelson, 11
Archer, Elizabeth, 186
Arlington Heights, Illinois, 158-159
Armstrong, Perry, 115

B

Bachelors Grove Cemetery, 52, 97, 157, 269
Baker, Frank M., 187
Barrington, Illinois, 157-158
Basa, Teresita, 253-255
Belknap, Myrtle, 289
Belushi, John, 39
Beverly, 5, 35, 134
Beverly Unitarian Church, 35
Billy Goat Tavern, 38-40
Biograph Theater, 279
Blair Witch Project, The, 51-53
Boy Scouts of America, Chicago Area, 218-221
Boyington, Philomena, 185-186
Boyington, William W., 185
Brighton Theater, 279
Britt, Alice, 31
Bronzeville, 134
Bryant, William Cullen, 192
Bucktown, 5, 11, 199-200
Bucktown Pub, 198-200

Buczkowske, Pamela, 232-233
Buena Park, 163
Burtan, Isabelle, 151-154

C

Calvary Cemetery, 273
Camp Fort Dearborn, 218, 220-221
Campbell Avenue, 5, 128-130
Cantigny, 81-82
Capone, Al, 6, 28-31, 110, 225
Captain Midnight, 148
Caray, Harry, 40
Chamberlain, Everett, 203-204
Channing Elementary School, 224-226
Channing Park, 226
Chicago American, 193-194
Chicago Cubs, 39-41
Chicago Daily News, The, 5, 128
Chicago Fire, 203-206, 237
Chicago Historical Society, 75
Chicago Park District, 163
Chicago River, 58-59, 75, 179, 237
Chicago Stock Yards, 140
Chicago Sun-Times, 226
Chicago Times, 203-204
Chicago Tribune, 81, 263
Chief Che-Che-Pin-Quay, 52
Chief Meachelle, 116
Chinatown, 75
Chua, Remy, 253-254
Cigrand, Emmeline, 291
City Cemetery, 175, 273
clairvoyance, 139, 191
Clark, James, 31

S

T

U

Ursula Bielski grew up in a haunted house on Chicago's North Side. At an early age she became a believer in paranormal experiences, from the curse of the Chicago Cubs at nearby Wrigley Field to the hauntings at local Graceland Cemetery by a nineteenth-century ghost girl. Underscoring these neighborhood folk tales were accounts by her police officer father of personal encounters with Big Foot and no less than the devil himself.

As an undergraduate at Benedictine University, Bielski was able to explore the interplay of belief and experience, focusing her coursework on the relationship between science and religion. Outside the classroom she tagged along with psychology students investigating reported cases of haunting phenomena which took her to such notorious sites as the Country House Restaurant in suburban Clarendon Hills; Chicago's Red Lion Pub; and the Oshkosh Opera House (Wisconsin). Her fascination with the methodology and philosophy of *psi* research led her to more structured work in the field of parapsychology.

As a graduate student at Northeastern Illinois University, Bielski explored related aspects of American intellectual and cultural history, particularly the Spiritualist movement of the nineteenth century and its transformation into psychical research and parapsychology. As a student affiliate of the Parapsychological Association, an international body dedicated to *psi* research, Bielski was a frequent contributor to the group's bulletin.

Intrigued by the apparent relationship between folklore and paranormal experience, Bielski eventually turned her interests toward her hometown, penning her acclaimed and widely successful book, *Chicago Haunts: Ghostlore of the Windy City.* After several printings of the book and the release of a second edition, Bielski now lectures regularly on the subject, having emerged as an expert on Chicago's spiritual netherworld. In 1999, she teamed up with cemetery photographer Matt Hucke to write *Graveyards of Chicago: The People, History, Art, and Lore of Cook County Cemeteries.*

Bielski is the editor of *PA News*, the quarterly bulletin of the Parapsychology Association. She has recently finished a children's book, *Creepy Chicago*, and is working on the development of a Spanish language and an audiobook version of *Chicago Haunts.* She lives in Chicago with her husband, author David Cowan, and their daughters.

OTHER LAKE CLAREMONT PRESS BOOKS

MORE FROM URSULA BIELSKI

Chicago Haunts: Ghostlore of the Windy City
by Ursula Bielski
Bielski captures over 160 years of Chicago's haunted history with her distinctive blend of lively storytelling, in-depth historical research, exclusive interviews, and insights from parapsychology. Called "a masterpiece of the genre," "a must-read," and "an absolutely first-rate-book" by reviewers, *Chicago Haunts* continues to earn the praise of critics and readers alike.
0-9642426-7-2, October 1998, softcover, 277 pages, 29 photos, $15

Graveyards of Chicago:
The People, History, Art, and Lore of Cook County Cemeteries
by Matt Hucke and Ursula Bielski
Discover a Chicago that exists just beneath the surface—about six feet under!
0-9642426-4-8, November 1999, softcover, 228 pages, 168 photos, $15

MORE GHOSTS

Haunted Michigan: Recent Encounters with Active Spirits
by Rev. Gerald S. Hunter
Hunter shares his investigations into modern ghost stories—active hauntings that continue to this day—and uncovers a chilling array of local spirits in his tour of the two peninsulas.
1-893121-10-0, October 2000, softcover, 207 pages, 20 photos, $12.95

More Haunted Michigan:
New Encounters with Ghosts of the Great Lakes State
by Rev. Gerald S. Hunter
1-893121-29-1, Fall 2002, softcover, approx. 200 pages, photos, $15

REGIONAL HISTORY

Chicago's Midway Airport: The First Seventy-Five Years
by Christopher Lynch
Midway was Chicago's first official airport, and for decades it was the busiest airport in the nation, and then the world. Its story is a reflection of America, encompassing heroes and villains, generosity and greed, boom and bust, progress and decline, and in the final analysis, rebirth. A celebration of the rich history of an airport and a window to an earlier era.
1-893121-18-6, Fall 2002, oblong, larger format softcover, approx. 250 pages, 180 historic photos, $19.95

The Hoofs and Guns of the Storm: Chicago's Civil War Connections
by Arnie Bernstein, with foreword by Senator Paul Simon
Far from the Mason-Dixon line, Chicago and Chicagoans were involved in the War Between the States in ways now often overlooked. Before visiting Gettysburg, Mississippi, or Virginia, use Bernstein's history and guidebook to appreciate the historical tourism available right outside your door! Includes Lincoln sites.
1-893121-06-2, Fall 2002, softcover, approx. 350 pages, historic photos, $15.95

Near West Side Stories:
Struggles for Community in Chicago's Maxwell Street Neighborhood
by Carolyn Eastwood
Recommended by *Chicago* magazine! A current and ongoing story of unequal power in Chicago. Four representatives of immigrant and migrant groups that have had a distinct territorial presence in the Halsted/Roosevelt area of the Near West Side—one Jewish, one Italian, one African-American, and one Mexican—reminisce fondly on life in the old neighborhood and tell of their struggles to save it and the 120-year-old Maxwell Street Market that was at its core.
1-893121-09-7, June 2002, softcover, 360 pages, 113 historic and contemporary photos, $17.95

Great Chicago Fires: Historic Blazes That Shaped a City
by David Cowan
As Chicago changed from agrarian outpost to industrial giant, it would be visited time and again by some of the worst infernos in American history—fires that sparked not only banner headlines but, more importantly, critical upgrades in fire safety laws across the globe. Acclaimed author (*To Sleep With the Angels*) and veteran firefighter David Cowan tells the story of the other "great" Chicago fires, noting the causes, consequences, and historical context of each. In transporting readers beyond the fireline and into the ruins, Cowan brings readers up close to the heroism, awe, and devastation generated by the fires that shaped Chicago.
1-893121-07-0, August 2001, oblong, larger format softcover, 167 pages, 80 historic photos, $19.95

The Chicago River: A Natural and Unnatural History
by Libby Hill
Hill presents an intimate biography of a humble, even sluggish, stream in the right place at the right time—the story of the making and perpetual re-making of a river by everything from geological forces to the interventions of an emerging and mighty city. Winner of the 2001 American Regional History Publishing Award (1st Place, Midwest) and the 2000 Midwest Independent Publishers Association Award (2nd Place, History).
1-893121-02-X, August 2000, softcover, 302 pages, 78 maps and photos, $16.95

Literary Chicago: A Book Lover's Tour of the Windy City
by Greg Holden, with foreword by Harry Mark Petrakis
Chicago has attracted and nurtured writers, editors, publishers, and book lovers for more than a century and continues to be one of the nation's liveliest literary cities. Join Holden as he journeys through the places, people, ideas, events, and culture of Chicagoland's historic and contemporary literary world. Includes 11 detailed

walking/driving tours.

1-893121-01-1, March 2001, softcover, 332 pages, 83 photos, 11 maps, $15.95

"The Movies Are":
Carl Sandburg's Film Reviews and Essays, 1920-1928
Ed. and with historical commentary by Arnie Bernstein, intro. by Roger Ebert
During the 1920s, a time when movies were still considered light entertainment by
most newspapers, the *Chicago Daily News* gave Sandburg a unique forum to express
his views on the burgeoning film arts. *"The Movies Are"* compiles hundreds of
Sandburg's writings on film, including reviews, interviews, and his earliest
published essays of Abraham Lincoln—which he wrote for his film column. Take a
new look at one of Hollywood's most exciting periods through the critical
perspective of one of America's great writers, a passionate film advocate who began
defining the scope and sophistication of future film criticism.

1-893121-05-4, October 2000, softcover, 397 pages, 72 historic photos, $17.95

Hollywood on Lake Michigan: 100 Years of Chicago and the Movies
by Arnie Bernstein, with foreword by *Soul Food* writer/director George Tillman, Jr.
Our editor's favorite! A history and street guide that finally gives Chicago and
Chicagoans due credit for their prominent role in moviemaking history, from the
silent era to the present. With trivia, special articles, historic and contemporary
photos, film profiles, anecdotes, and exclusive interviews with dozens of
personalities, including Studs Terkel, Roger Ebert, Gene Siskel, Dennis Franz,
Harold Ramis, Joe Mantegna, Bill Kurtis, Irma Hall, and Tim Kazurinsky. Winner of
the 2000 American Regional History Publishing Award (1st Place, Midwest).

0-9642426-2-1, December 1998, softcover, 364 pages, 80 photos, $15

REGIONAL TRAVEL &
GUIDEBOOKS BY LOCALS

A Cook's Guide to Chicago: Where to Find Everything
You Need and Lots of Things You Didn't Know You Did
by Marilyn Pocius
Pocius shares the culinary expertise she acquired in chef school and through years of
footwork around the city searching for the perfect ingredients and supplies. Each
section includes store listings, cooking tips, and "Top 10 ingredients" lists to give
readers a jump start on turning their kitchens into dens of worldly cuisine. Includes
an easy-to-use index with over 2,000 ingredients!

1-893121-16-X, June 2002, softcover, 275 pages, $15

Ticket to Everywhere: The Best of *Detours* Travel Column
by Dave Hoekstra, with foreword by Studs Terkel
66 of *Chicago Sun-Times* columnist Dave Hoekstra's best road trip explorations into
the offbeat people, places, events, and history of the greater Midwest and Route 66
areas.

1-893121-11-9, November 2000, softcover, 227 pages, 70 photos, 9 maps, $15.95

A Native's Guide to Chicago, 4th Edition
by Lake Claremont Press, edited by Sharon Woodhouse
Venture into the nooks and crannies of everyday Chicago with this one-of-a-kind, comprehensive budget guide. Over 400 pages of free, inexpensive, and unusual things to do in the Windy City make this the perfect resource for tourists, business travelers, visiting suburbanites, and resident Chicagoans. Called the "best guidebook for locals" in *New City*'s "Best of Chicago" issue!
1-893121-23-2, January 2003, softcover, photos and maps, $15.95

A Native's Guide to Northwest Indiana
by Mark Skertic
0-9642426-8-0, January 2003, softcover, photos, maps, $15

A Native's Guide to Chicago's Northern Suburbs
by Jason Fargo
0-9642426-8-0, June 1999, softcover, 207 pages, photos, maps, $12.95

A Native's Guide to Chicago's Northwest Suburbs
by Martin A. Bartels
1-893121-00-3, August 1999, softcover, 315 pages, photos, maps, $12.95

A Native's Guide to Chicago's Western Suburbs
by Laura Mazzuca Toops and John W. Toops, Jr.
0-9642426-6-4, August 1999, softcover, 210 pages, photos, maps, $12.95

A Native's Guide to Chicago's South Suburbs
by Christina Bultinck and Christy Johnston-Czarnecki
0-9642426-1-3, June 1999, softcover, 242 pages, photos, maps, $12.95

Discounts when you order multiple copies!
2 books—10% off total, 3–4 books—20% off,
5–9 books—25% off, 10+ books—40% off

—Low shipping fees—
$2 for the first book and $.50 for each additional book, with a maximum charge of $5.

Order by mail, phone, fax, or e-mail.
All of our books have a no-hassle, 100% money back guarantee.

Pay with check, money order, Visa, or MasterCard.

4650 N. Rockwell St.
Chicago, IL 60625
773/583-7800
773/583-7877 (fax)
lcp@lakeclaremont.com
www.lakeclaremont.com

LAKE CLAREMONT PRESS

ALSO BY LAKE CLAREMONT PRESS

Chicago Haunts:
Ghostlore of the Windy City
by Ursula Bielski

Graveyards of Chicago:
The People, History, Art, and Lore
of Cook County Cemeteries
by Matt Hucke and Ursula Bielski

Haunted Michigan: Recent
Encounters with Active Spirits
by Rev. Gerald S. Hunter

More Haunted Michigan:
New Encounters with Ghosts
of the Great Lakes State
by Rev. Gerald S. Hunter.

Hollywood on Lake Michigan: 100
Years of Chicago and the Movies
by Arnie Bernstein

"The Movies Are":
Carl Sandburg's Film Reviews
and Essays, 1920-1928
ed. by Arnie Bernstein,
intro. by Roger Ebert

The Chicago River:
A Natural and Unnatural History
by Libby Hill

Literary Chicago: A Book Lover's
Tour of the Windy City
by Greg Holden

Ticket to Everywhere: The Best of
Detours Travel Column
by Dave Hoekstra,
foreword by Studs Terkel

Great Chicago Fires: Historic
Blazes That Shaped a City
by David Cowan

Near West Side Stories: Struggles
for Community in Chicago's
Maxwell Street Neighborhood
by Carolyn Eastwood

Chicago's Midway Airport:
The First Seventy-Five Years
by Christopher Lynch

A Cook's Guide to Chicago
by Marilyn Pocius

COMING SOON

Creepy Chicago (for kids!)
by Ursula Bielski

Muldoon: A True Chicago Ghost
Story: Tales of a Haunted Rectory
by Rocco and Dan Facchini

The Hoofs and Guns of the Storm:
Chicago's Civil War Connections
by Arnie Bernstein

A Native's Guide to
Northwest Indiana
by Mark Skertic

A Native's Guide to Chicago,
4th Edition
ed. by Sharon Woodhouse

The Firefighter's Best Friend:
Lives and Legends of
Chicago Firehouse Dogs
by Trevor and Drew Orsinger

The Politics of Recreation
by Charles Shaw